What people are saying about Beatrice Bruno, The Drill Sergeant of Life, and her books ---

We all have excuses for who we are. The hardest one to touch is our childhood. In *How to Get Over Yourself and Let Go of the P.A.S.T.*, Beatrice Bruno gives real steps to address and *"Get Over…"* what was to achieve a stronger what is.

Diana Hall
The Speaking Author
www.SpeakingAuthor.com

Just recently I met Beatrice Bruno. Her enthusiasm and honesty bowled me over. She is such a dynamic person I could hardly wait to read her book, "***How to Get Over Yourself, Get Out of Your Own Way, and Get What You Want Out of Life!***' Now, having read the book, I'm even more impressed. It makes so much sense! She makes it so simple. I am already applying some of the principles she teaches. Can hardly wait to hear her speak and attend a workshop with her. God Bless her and what her book will do for people.

LuWanda Ford,
Chairman and Founder,
Pocket Flag Project

Beatrice Bruno's book, ***How To Get Over Yourself, Get Out of Your Own Way and Get What YOU Want Out of Life!*** is a great tool for anyone who has experienced a loss of passion. Beatrice digs into people's worlds, forcing them to confront what they have been standing in the way of - and then encourages them to create newly - both by focusing on the path and by letting go of the all the things that will not keep us on the path. This is a life-affirming book that will open up new possibilities for many people!

*--**Mary Camacho,***
Author of The Internet Plan

How To Get Over Yourself
and
Let Go of the Past!

Beatrice Bruno, The Drill Sergeant of Life

Unattributed quotations are by Beatrice Bruno.

Unless otherwise indicated, Scripture quotations are from the King James Version of the Holy Bible.

Published by Heard Word Publishing, LLC
1980 Van Buren Way
Aurora, CO 80011

How To Get Over Yourself and Let Go of the Past!

ISBN – 13: **978-0-9801060-5-3**

These and other books by Beatrice Bruno are available at www.TheGetOverItGal.com.

For info on booking The Drill Sergeant of Life to speak at your event or for more info on *The Get Over Yourself BootCamps*, contact Beatrice at Beatrice@TheGetOverItGal.com.

DEDICATION

This book is dedicated to the M.O.O.D. Squad (Move Over or Dance!) Susan, Helen, Evangelist Ruth Williams from Denver, Colorado; Angela from Queens, New York; Carolyn from Clarksville, Tennessee, and Apostle Mary Braswell from McKinney, Texas.

Each of us is in the process of Getting Over Ourselves. We are not afraid to learn something new and scary about ourselves in the process. As we learn to let go of the past, we realize that our future is far brighter than what we know.

Thanks to the M.O.O.D. Squad for keeping it REAL!!!

CONTENTS

ACKNOWLEDGMENTS

Jesus said, I am the Way, the Truth, and the Life. No one comes to the Father but by Me.

To Thine be the glory, and the honor, and the power forever, and ever! Amen

If it were not for the Lord, this book would not have reached this stage. Therefore, I thank Almighty God alone for all He has done, all He is doing, and ALL He will do as He takes me through the process of being ALL He has called me to be. He alone is my Rock!

DISCLAIMER:

This book is the second in a series of books designed to help the reader Get Over Him- or Herself, Get Out of His or Her Own Way, and Get What He or She Wants Out of Life.

During a journey which is entering its third year, I am continually discovering who I truly am and who God has created me to be. Every day is a new day of insight and revelation as God Almighty opens more doors and shows to me the person He sees in His Own eyes.

I will not say that this is the end of this particular journey, though. The Lord has already revealed at least two more books in the series. I don't know how long the series is; neither do I know the depth of teachings He will download through me for the purpose of helping His people.

So, stay tuned. There is more to come!

THE DRILL SERGEANT

FOREWORD

When people hear that I am the Pastor of the Drill Sergeant of Life, **they** get very excited; **I**, on the other hand, get overwhelmed because that means they expect me to have something valuable to offer to them. The higher the Drill Sergeant's rise, **and she is rising fast**, the more pressure I feel. Some people think that I have something to do with her impeccable skills as a motivator and public speaker. Truthfully, all I did was encourage her to follow God.

This is the second book I have been asked to write the foreword to that has been written by another exceptional person whom I have the privilege to lead. When first asked, the thoughts in my head were, *"Why would anyone want **me** to write the foreword for their book?"*

I questioned myself. As a matter of fact, I continue to say things to myself like, " *I'm just a small time Pastor. My credentials to endorse a book are nothing compared to others who are more qualified."*

Doesn't that sound so foolish? Who wants to read the foreword from someone who thinks so little of himself like that? **I don't!**

It wasn't even that I thought little of myself, though. Anyone who knows me understands that I thrive in confidence! Though I am 5 foot 6 in physical stature, in my mind, I'd say I am about 6 foot 7. I do things that others feel impossible or are too afraid to do.

When I was 26, I travelled to Kenya, by myself, to preach for a friend of mine and do some missionary work. Everyone thought I was crazy! I barely knew the man I was going to see. I had never been out of the country with the exception of a Caribbean cruise I was privileged to go on as a teenager. However, to travel internationally, not knowing the rules or expectations of foreign governments, on my own, was, in many people's eyes, insane.

Needless to say, I had a great trip. I spoke in front of the largest crowds of people I had ever seen before. Miracles took place; people were healed of cancer and many other serious and life-threatening diseases. I was afforded the opportunity to feed orphans and meet a lot of wonderful people. All in all, the trip was a success! All those who had negative things to say rejoiced greatly upon my return and at the news of my adventures.

Suffice it to say, I have always been daring and willing to do things that others seem to fear.

That having been said, I must say, when Beatrice Bruno, The Drill Sergeant of Life asked me to write the foreword for this book, *How To Get Over Yourself and Let Go of the P.A.S.T.*, I was nervous. After reading this book, I now know *why*.

Thank God I read this book! It has made me look at myself in ways I had never considered. I realize now that there were things in my past I had not truly released.

Like an old girlfriend who still lingers in your heart, you know that it's over and you both have moved on. But, you secretly wish things had gone differently. It's that secret wish of something that never will be that keeps you bound to the past and impairs your future.

I have led people for many years as a pastor. I have prayed for people in hospitals. I have performed both weddings and funerals. I have provided counsel and comfort. However, in all of that, I wasn't happy. Don't get me wrong; I enjoyed doing it. But, I wasn't happy because I felt like a failure the whole time.

The people I helped would get through their problems and leave our church for the big one down the street. I struggled to provide for my own family. I encouraged everyone else to have faith in God, all the while having a hard time trusting God myself.

I felt just like a vending machine. People walked up to me, slid in a few coins, selected what they wanted and left; only to return when they wanted something else. And if what they desired was not available, they stormed away, disgruntled. At least I had the coins they deposited right? Nope! Someone else came along and emptied that as well.

Don't get me wrong; I am a great speaker. People come from all around to hear me share the Word of the Lord. I also love helping people, but did not personally benefit from the labor I was putting forth.

I became the bad guy for people who needed someone to blame for their troubles. Yet at the same time, I was their hero when they needed some advice or comfort. I **hated** doing what I **loved** to do. **People** made me angry, and I felt stuck.

Then, the most tragic event of all happened; my baby daughter died. There was no warning; she died shortly after her birth. It was terrible! All I could do then was try to bury myself in my work. I was devastated and didn't even know it. Didn't matter though; I had a church to build. So, I took one week off and kept preaching. Six months later, it all came crumbling down.

We lost our church building, our members were leaving, my wife was depressed, and I was seriously ill. The sad part in all this is that I didn't even realize how messed up I was. To make a long, sad story really short, I finally took a break.

During that time, I prayed and sought God's direction. He told me that I was doing everything for everybody else and nothing for myself. He also told me that, if I didn't take care of myself, I couldn't be a good husband to my wife, a good father to my son, nor a good leader to the people I pastor.

So, I relaxed more. I stopped doing everything myself. I did only what I was supposed to do and began doing more recreational things that I enjoy. Things got a bit better and I settled into a simple life of ministry.

However, after reading this book, I had an epiphany. I discovered that, although I am currently experiencing the best times of ministry I ever have, again, I'm not enjoying it. This time though, not for the same reasons.

There are people in my congregations who think very highly of me. They have been so influenced by my teaching, they consider me an answer to prayer. There are people all around me now that I have pushed and encouraged to stay focused on God and follow Him. They are stepping into their true purpose and love me for it. In almost two decades of ministry, I have never had a group of people who actually appreciated me and I am just realizing this.

Because of my past experiences in ministry, I was conditioned to just settle in and serve people; it became a mere job. After reading what The Drill Sergeant of Life had to say in ***How To Get Over Yourself and Let Go of the P.A.S.T.***, I realized that I hadn't gotten over myself yet. Nor had I let go of my past experiences as a pastor.

I am a much better Pastor now than I was then. I am actually succeeding and experiencing blessing; but, I did not know it because my past still had me... and I it.

You can't enjoy the benefits of a new relationship if your old girlfriend haunts the attic of your mind and heart. Somehow the failure mentality of my previous pastoral days still occupied space in my heart and mind. I had to reevaluate my life.

I did a 360-degree turn to find out how this failure mentality had gotten filed in my future expectations. Once I found the malfunction, I fired the whole thought process and tossed that old failure mentality file into the ***Round File of Life*** ®...The TRASH!!

This whole book has blessed my life tremendously! As with all things, there will be certain parts which stand out to some more than others; but, everyone will be greatly benefitted.

For me, **Chapter 11** is of particular note. My problem was that I needed to change how I viewed my past. Before, I was upset when people left our church to go to another. Now, I am grateful to have served that person for the season he or she was with us. God used me to help these precious people grow so they can now better serve the churches they currently attend.

The improper view I had of my past corrupted the outlook of my future. Therefore, when Beatrice asked me to write the foreword for this book, I felt as though my thoughts would not be worthy. I felt less than how she viewed me. I couldn't dare imagine that someone wanted my words to precede their own in a book that will touch the world! I didn't see myself as a foreword writer; I saw myself as a small time pastor. But I now know that I have always been much more than that!

I have chosen to bare my all before you today; I hope that you hear the essence of my words. Beatrice Bruno, The Drill Sergeant of Life, has written a book, ***How To Get Over Yourself and Let Go of the P.A.S.T.***, that has greatly impacted my life. It has helped me lay aside some destructive patterns which I, like many of you, subconsciously harbored. I have let go of the past, and now I can apprehend and fully embrace my future success!

Thank You, Drill Sergeant!

Your Friend and Pastor

Adrian Taylor, Jr.

How To Get Over Yourself and Let Go of the Past!

PHASE I
Forget What Is Behind

Chapter 1 - If You're Holding On To Your Past...

You can't grab hold of your future. Think about this: if you hold on to something tightly with both hands, how will you grab hold of something that someone else is trying to give to you? You can't!

Everyone has had problems and made mistakes in their lives. If we were honest with ourselves, we would admit that we *still* have problems and *still* make mistakes. But, to progress, move forward, we have to see these problems and mistakes as not insurmountable. These problems and mistakes are things that make us grow and help us mature in our purpose. There is no getting around this fact.

Now, as we deal with our problems, of course, others come and sweetly confirm that we *have* problems and make mistakes. *How kind they are!*

You see, this is one of the ways we are tripped up when we are going through. Other well-meaning (and some who are not so well-meaning) folks may come along side us and show us just how bad off we really are.

But, God has given us the way out of our past problems and mistakes. Is this book about religion? No. It's about truth and how we are able to **Let Go Of The Past** so we can move forward in our lives.

Life is similar to driving down a highway: if you continually look in the rearview mirror, you will soon crash into something. Take the same concept with life: if you always and only consider what happened in the past and don't move forward, you are destined to remain in the past and never be able to move forward into your true destiny.

Look at what Apostle Paul (whom I first introduced to you in *How To Get Over Yourself, Get Out of Your Own Way, and Get What YOU Want Out of Life!*) tells us in Philippians 3:12 – 15;

[1.Not as though I had already attained, either were already perfect]: [2. but I follow after, if that I may apprehend that for which also I am apprehended of Christ Jesus.] [3. Brethren, I count not myself to have apprehended] **but** *[4. this one thing I do], [5. forgetting those things which are behind] and [6. reaching forth unto those things which are before], [7. I press toward the mark for the prize of the high calling of God in Christ Jesus.]*

Now, as you can see, I have broken this verse down into seven sections. These seven sections are elements, if you will, to letting go of your past so that you can claim the future for which you are destined. Around these seven elements, I have built seven life-changing keys that you can implement to **Get Over Yourself and Let Go of the Past!**

OK, let's move forward. By the time Paul wrote this letter to the Church of Philippi, he was seasoned in the ways of the Lord and was rocking and rolling in the Spirit of God. He had been taught, and had learned by the experiences God allowed him to have, that he could not hold on to his past if he wanted to move forward in what his Creator had for him.

Probing Questions to Free Your Mind

1	What are some of the things you really need to let go of so you can move forward toward your destiny?
2	What is the main reason you still hold on to these things?
3	What steps have you taken or need to take to release these things from your life?

Take a few moments to answer these questions. Really probe your mind for the answers. Don't just give an answer so you can continue to read and see what comes next. If you have to, answer the questions, leave them for a day and then come back. This is about you. You need to know the answers to these questions.

You must be willing to probe deeply so you can remove the clutter that has kept you from moving forward for so long.

When you probe, it will hurt. It will disturb you and cause you to want to put this book down! **Keep reading!** You will find something to help; I promise!

Now, let me share an acronym with you: **P³.A.S.T.** – **P**eople, **P**laces, **P**ossibilities **A**nd **S**ituations **T**erminated.

We really need to consider our P³.A.S.T. and what it means in our forward movement. You see, without ever realizing it, most people hold on to their past; it is comfortable and allows them to keep from moving forward.

What?!?!?!

Yes! You see, our past is like an old friend. That old friend convinces us that we have already achieved a certain level of mediocrity. Now, don't be offended, but that certain level of mediocrity or passivity feels good. It causes us to remain where we are so that new stuff - new opportunities or new situations - will not cause us to be *un*comfortable.

One of my favorite quotes from my first book of this series is, *Failure is comfortable; success is uncomfortable.* Unless we step out of our comfort zone and step out of our past, we will not give ourselves the opportunity to finally succeed in life!

Your **P³.A.S.T.** always waits to draw you back in. You see, your past is just as comfortable with you as you are with it. As a matter of fact, it is more comfortable because it has a lot more to lose than you do. Sounds crazy? Well, believe me; it's true.

Let me share something with you from my past. From when I was a teen until I was a young adult, I did a lot of crazy, self-destructive stuff. I had this really destructive nature aimed at myself because I had very low self-esteem and just didn't believe in me.

After entering the Army, I stayed away from the town I grew up in and the people I grew up with. I remembered all the bad stuff, stupid stuff, I had done when I was younger.

I didn't realize at the time that all that old stuff kept me locked into my **P³.A.S.T.** Every so often, I revisited my thoughts and memories. I basically convinced myself that everything that had ever been said about me was true.

Well, a couple of years ago, I reconnected with some folks I had graduated with. You know what they said to me?

"You were the smartest, most intelligent out of all of us!"

"We expected great things from you because you were always such a great person!"

That just about blew my mind!

You see, these were the positive folks I had hung out with. But, I thought everyone thought the same about me. I had allowed those perceptions to hold me captive so that I couldn't become who I had been created to be.

As a matter of fact, these precious folks I had reconnected with were **P**eople **A**nd **S**ituations I was **T**hankful for! These were people I **needed** in my corner who would help me move forward into my destiny.

However, there were other **P**eople, **P**laces, **P**ossibilities **A**nd **S**ituations I **T**erminated because they were also **T**oxic in my life.

What we must remember going forward and growing into our destiny is just what Apostle Paul said: *Not as though I had already attained, either were already perfect.*

One thing I learned growing up in South Carolina; we are all imperfect people in an imperfect world. Not all **P**eople will be our friends; not all **P**laces will be good for us; not all **P**ossibilities will garner the success we desire.

I have learned, especially of late, that I am not perfect. As hard as I may try to be perfect in everything I do, the fact of the matter is that it just doesn't happen.

But, I also learned that the Lord God Almighty does not expect me to be perfect; He just wants me to be willing. He wants me to be willing to go through and grow through everything so that I may reach the level of excellence that He wants me to attain.

And so, I willingly go forward to attain the destiny I have been created for. Now, just as I did, we all need to consider our **P³.A.S.T.** We need to think about what it means in our forward movement.

If we combine our acronym, **P³.A.S.T.**, with Philippians 3:12 – 15, we will find that they work perfectly in conjunction with each other.

Paul realized that, although he had come a long way from where he previously was, he was not perfect. Yet, at no juncture do we actually witness Paul ever attempting to be perfect. He acknowledged that he had attained many things; perfection was not one of those things!

In our **P³.A.S.T.**, there are **P**eople, **P**laces, and **P**ossibilities that never quite made it to fruition. Since you are in a new season, you can stop trying to apprehend or capture those **P**eople, **P**laces, and **P**ossibilities and allow God to move you forward into your season of purpose right now.

And, believe it or not, ***you*** need to allow yourself to move forward as well. Remember, the **P³.A.S.T.** is your comfort zone. Everything about you feels comfortable there. You have to *break free* in order to *move forward*.

7

If you hold on to the People, Places, and Possibilities of your previous seasons, you will never fully realize the people or divine connections waiting in your new season; the places you will be allowed to travel to; or, the possibilities of an even greater future than what you had in the past. Let's explore some of those people.

Have you ever wondered why certain folks come into your life for a season and then abruptly leave? Or, maybe you attempted to establish a relationship and there just didn't seem to be much interest on either side? Or, have you ever had a person come into your life and you picked up on something causing you to flee before they could get their claws into you?

I have had relationships with folks that ended so abruptly, it gave me pause to think or question whether I had been the cause of their sudden departure from my life. But later, after thinking about it, I saw where God had actually allowed that person to come in for just a minute to show me something that I could learn from and write about.

Then, there were those I attempted to start a relationship with; before too long, we both seemed to lose interest. Now, to be honest, instances like this are very few and far in between for me. I have gotten into the habit of really scrutinizing folks coming into my life. You see, I can't be friends with everyone that approaches me. That may seem kind of cold or cruel, but there are some things you need to take into consideration.

We are not all in the same season of our lives. What do I mean by that? Well, there are seasons in which we will be called to be really close with others outside of our immediate families. We will be allowed to embrace and become emotionally involved with folks that cross our paths.

Then, we will experience seasons in which we will have a passing association with others. We will encounter these folks but may only establish a business or platonic relationship for whatever reason.

And, then, there will be yet other times when we won't even have a relationship with another. During these times, we will be required to keep to ourselves as we develop into the person we are destined to be. Sometimes, it is best that we pull away from others for a season so we can grow into our destiny. To learn more about this, contact me at Beatrice@TheGetOverItGal.com.

Now, there are also those who will come into your life and you will literally run from them. What? Oh, yea! Recently, I met a woman who, upon first meeting, seemed very sincere. I thought we would have a pretty good friendship. Then, I picked up on several things telling me, in no uncertain terms, that I would have to let this lady go!

The first thing I noticed was that she was quick to tell me **ALL** of her business! At first, I took the pastoral stand and gave her counsel. The more I counseled, the more she told! She called and dumped, called and dumped. Before I knew it, I was bogged down with her problems. Then, she wanted me to tell her about my business. I think you know that this wasn't going to happen!

Next, she borrowed money from me. Now, I don't mind helping folks out; I have had enough folks helping me in the past. But, I have also learned to release the money so there will be no hard feelings. This lady borrowed several times and would have continued had I not put a kibosh on it.

Now, let me share this with you. I returned to Colorado from New York in January 2011 after being there for a little over a year taking care of my dad and being in exile with the Lord. As I prepared to return to Denver, the Lord told me to not become emotionally entangled with anyone outside of my family and my close sphere. Now I know exactly why He warned me about this.

You see, when you become emotionally entangled with others outside of your immediate family and sphere, you can be drained quite rapidly and frequently and not have what you need to perform and accomplish your purpose. I had to release this lady, as well as others, from my life because she drained me.

Now, that's not to say that she or others like her will not enter my life again in the future; perhaps to stay for a little longer than what I allowed before. As a matter of fact, I know that the Lord will bring some folks back into my life.

Others I don't know. I am still waiting to see if He will allow our relationship to continue or if He has decided that the liaison has fulfilled its purpose for that particular season in my life. As of this writing, we have not had further contact.

But, please bear this in mind: even the worse relationships are not the easiest to come out of. I have had the most difficulty coming out of situations and relationships that were totally toxic; but, these relationships were totally comfortable as well.

When you are plagued by low or poor self-esteem, the worst relationship feels good to you; any port in a storm so to speak. The relationships I found the easiest to come out of, though, were those which I immediately recognized as not a good fit. I didn't allow them to get to second base so there was no harm, no foul.

How about you? Do you have difficulty leaving toxic relationships? Is it because you are comfortable or afraid you will look like the bad guy if you leave?

The Drill Sergeant of Life says: *Get Over Yourself and Let Go of the Past Relationship that could quite possibly be hindering you from moving forward into relationships that are more beneficial!*

Now, what about past places? Where are you right now in the whole scheme of things? What place are you at mentally, emotionally, or spiritually? Is this the place you should be in right now? Are there some places you previously visited that you need to let go of in this season of your life? We all have those places.

Mental anguish. Turmoil. Self-defeat. These are the places, if you will, or states for that matter, that we have to force ourselves to release or vacate from our lives right now. If we don't, eventually these places will defeat all we are attempting to accomplish.

Breathing Exercise – Free Your Mind and Fill With Good

Inhale deeply! Exhale completely!

Inhale deeply! Exhale completely!

How do you release the People and Places from your past? Repeat these vows:

*I release (*fill in the name or thing*) from my life right now!*

*I refuse to live in the state of (*confusion, indecision, anger, etc.*) anymore!*

I choose to move forward into the new season of my life!

Repeat out loud as many times during the day as you need to get into your spirit or subconscious. Proclaim it with fervor! Create vows that mean something to you.

You see, you need to mean it. You must be convicted about this; if not, you will slip back to those same type of people and the same state you were in before.

When we hold on to the past, this action diminishes our power from going forth into our future. We have to be careful of the power-stealers we allow to take over in our lives.

Now, let's discuss past possibilities. These are a problem sometimes. You see, our minds tend to lock on shoulda, woulda, coulda, or gonna and not necessarily in that order.

I coulda been somebody if...

I woulda done that if...

I shoulda gone to... but...

I was gonna do that… but…

These are power-stealers! They come along disguised as well-meaning supportive friends but are anything but! These past possibilities plague your mind and heart. They bombard you with *'what ifs'* and other repetitive utterances that cause you to question your ability to move forward.

And that is one thing we must never allow to happen. We were created to move forward! We were not created to stagnate or stand still. We are to progress in and through every stage of our lives and mature into the next stage.

Let me ask this? If you planted, say, a strawberry patch, what would you do if nothing ever grew in the patch? Granted, the first year would probably be very sparse. You would tend it, fertilizing it in anticipation of the coming strawberry season, right?

Then, the next season comes and no strawberries! How long would you continue to labor receiving nothing for your labor? Not very long, I imagine. You would do one of two things: turn over the soil and start over again or cross growing strawberries off your list.

Well, those past possibilities are either going to produce or not! Don't waste your time on *shoulda, woulda, coulda or gonna* when you could just move forward into the possibilities of this season and reach the destiny you were created to reach.

There are also situations and circumstances we need to Terminate. They are over and done with just like the non-producing strawberry patch. They have no more control or effect in our lives. Unfortunately, we allow the majority of these situations and circumstances to repeat and keep us in the same mindset we have always had.

Instead of allowing these situations and circumstances to dictate our future, put them in proper perspective and move forward. Try the following examples on for size. First, I will give the negative action; then, I will give you the response for that action.

And remember; **YOU Are Not Your P³.A.S.T.!**

Say that with conviction: I AM NOT MY PAST!!!

I was raped when I was a child.
    I survived sexual molestation and am mentally and emotionally whole.

I was abandoned by my _____.
    I survived abandonment and am now embraced.

I was rejected by _____.
    I survived rejection and am accepted.

I was abused.
    I survived abuse and am now loved.

I was domestically violated.
    I survived domestic violence and am now stable in my environment.

We all have experienced abuse and mistreatment in our lives. As hard or difficult as it may seem, it is up to us to not stay there. We cannot continue to allow our past to abuse and mistreat us.

Let Go Of The Past so you can move forward into what you were created for.

D.S.ofL. Let Go of the P.A.S.T. Key #1

I'm Not Perfect But I'm Willing!

Living a life on purpose does not mean that you live a life of perfection. There are few things that are perfect in the world.

Some may eventually encounter the perfect job: after wading through a sea of imperfect jobs.

Some may observe a perfect sunset. But the perfect sunset has nothing to do with the person but everything to do with the Creator of the sunset: Almighty God.

Some may experience a perfect relationship; only after the disappointment of many failed relationships.

Don't worry so much about being perfect! Be willing to grow through each experience so you can reach the level of excellence you were created for.

Chapter 2 - Dwelling In The Past

Let's do a quick inventory of your spiritual or mental closet. Please check the box on the right to acknowledge that you have these things in your closet; things you need to take to the dump. Feel free to add any other items you find stored in this particular closet.

1	Hat of confusion	
2	Scarf of sorrow	
3	Cloak of worry	
4	Shoes of misdirection	
5	Past unanswered prayer requests	
6	Past problems	

Many of us have a problem. I invite you to look into your spiritual closet for a moment; what do you see? If your closet is cluttered with any, some, or all these things, how are you ever going to place something new and different in there if you keep it cluttered with the past?

I once heard the story of a lady who wanted a new couch for her living room. She also desired to have new curtains to match the couch. She kept hoping and praying for the new couch until one day a friend came over. Her friend asked where she was going to put the new furniture.

The woman looked at her friend as though she were crazy and answered, *"Well, right there where the old one is, of course!"*

Her friend then told her, *"Well, you need to get rid of the old to prepare for the new."*

To the woman, this sounded strange but she sensed an element of truth. So, she finally got rid of the old couch.

Now, instead of struggling, wondering how she would be able to afford a new couch, as soon as she released the old couch, her money lined up and she was able to receive a new couch. As soon as that happened, she began to rid herself of all the old she wanted to get rid of and replace with new.

Is there a moral here? Yes; if you continue to hold on to your past, how will your future ever find you? If you continue to hold on to what was or what didn't get off the ground, how will you ever grab onto what is and what will be?

Let's go back to our acronym for a bit. **P³.A.S.T.** – **P**eople, **P**laces, **P**ossibilities **A**nd **S**ituations **T**erminated.

The main definition for dwell is to live. You are living/ dwelling in the past if:

- You continually focus on the past.

- You focus more on what was than what is and what will be.
- You dredge up those things that you coulda, woulda shoulda done or are gonna do.

I also want to remind you of Philippians 3:12 – 15:

[1.Not as though I had already attained, either were already perfect]: [2. but I follow after, if that I may apprehend that for which also I am apprehended of Christ Jesus.] [3. Brethren, I count not myself to have apprehended] **but** *[4. this one thing I do], [5. forgetting those things which are behind] and [6. reaching forth unto those things which are before], [7. I press toward the mark for the prize of the high calling of God in Christ Jesus.]*

Something is following you. Something desires to overtake you and keep you in one of two places: either in your past or in your future.

Now, your past, as we discovered in Chapter One, is very comfortable with you. Over the years, you have been the best of friends; you have been the worst of friends. You have had fallouts; you have been frienemies. But, you have stuck with each other through thick and thin. Every time one of you tries to leave the other, you both find a way to make things work.

And so, you fell into a place of comfortable hatred. You hate the past. You hate staying with it but feel that you have no other choice. You settle for the relationship, as is, because you can't possibly do any better.

Along comes your future. Your future is determined to apprehend you. It goes to great lengths to establish a relationship; a lasting, productive, prosperous relationship which it knows you need. Your future pulls out all the stops, presenting you with People, Places, Possibilities And Situations that Tantalize you to strive for it.

But, your old friend, P³.A.S.T., continues to pull on you. He pulls out all the stops as well. He follows you around to make sure you know that he still cares and is still as comfortable as before. Now, though, you are confused.

You want the future and all it has to offer; but, the P³.A.S.T. has its greedy talons in you. What do you do?

Believe it or not, you need to have a garbage sale. You need to pack up all that P³.A.S.T. garbage (I'm calling it what it is!) and sell it. Don't hesitate! Pack that stuff up! Go into every closet in your dwelling place and pull out everything not relevant to your moving forward.

As a matter of fact, don't sell that stuff to someone else; **Take it to the garbage dump!** Box it up, cart it off, and dump it!

Be reminded of this: there is no future in your past if all you want to do is wallow in it. What do I mean by wallowing in it?

Well, if you find yourself going into that closet and playing dress-up with the contents, you are wallowing in your past. And, you have a problem.

You see, the more you wallow in it, the more you want to wallow in it. And the more you want to wallow in it, the more it has its clutches in and on you!

The past should always only serve as a reminder of who you were and what has already happened in your life. The past, your past, does not define who you are right now at this very moment.

Many folks wallow in their past and allow it to consume them for no other reason than that it is a very comfortable place to be. But, the more they wallow in it, the more it can claim of the person's heart and mind and will eventually consume the person. It will deceive him or her that this is where they should be.

NOT SO! You are **NOT** your past!

LET...   IT...   GO!!!

Don't get me wrong, though. In some instances, the past is referred to in a positive manner. In my first book of this series, *How To Get Over Yourself, Get Out of Your Own Way, and Get What YOU Want Out of Life!,* I referred to Michael Jackson whom we all knew and most loved. In this book, though, let's talk a little about another very popular Michael; Jordan, that is.

Michael Jordan is an excellent example of someone who used his past positively. As a matter of fact, he allowed his past to push him into the stratosphere as one of the most favorite athletes in his field.

But, look at what he says about himself: "*I've missed more than 9000 shots in my career. I've lost almost 300 games. 26 times, I've been trusted to take the game winning shot and missed! I've failed over and over again in my life. And that's why I succeed.*"

Mr. Jordan allowed his past to push him to being one of the best-known, trusted and respected athletes in the world. He could have allowed these same things to hinder his personal development but he did not. He pressed through and apprehended the greatness that apprehended him.

When Michael was in high school, he was cut from the varsity basketball team. He could have ended his basketball playing career at that point; many others did.

Instead, he allowed that experience to push him to be better than he had ever been before; and, we know the result of that.

He proved his first coaches wrong. He allowed his past to catapult him into a professional basketball playing future that few have achieved before him.

And there were many before him: Lew Alcindor aka Kareem Abdul Jabar, Walt Frazier, Wilt Chamberlain, Wes Unseld. All these men were rock-stars of basketball in their seasons. And, then there was Michael Jordan.

He came into his season, ran with the proverbial ball and never looked back. He is multi-talented and multi-faceted in golf as well as baseball. But basketball is his bread and butter.

Philippians 3:12 *But I follow after, if that I may apprehend that for which I am apprehended of Christ Jesus.*

Your future is hot on your trail! It is chasing you because it knows what is ahead for you. Look around yourself: have you noticed that the scenery has changed from what you once saw? Have you noticed that the people, places, and possibilities have become something new and different; something you've not experienced before?

You see, you were created for more than what your past will allow you to accomplish. All these years, you have sought something different while at the same time running back to that which was comfortable. Unfortunately, it accepted you and you it!

If I were to tell you that there is a future ahead of you that will cause your past to pale in comparison, what would you do? Would you go and box up all your past and take it to the dump? Would you make room for the new?

In my life, I have experienced the same as everyone else when dealing with my past. There have been times when I thought that all I would ever have were the past events I had already lived through; the past experiences that continued to recur in my life.

I never knew that in order for me to have the future I so desired, I would have to apprehend it and allow it to apprehend me. What do I mean by this? Check this out.

By calling or trade, I am a motivational speaker and author. This is something, a gift, I was created with. This gift is in my DNA, my physical/psychological mental and emotional makeup. I can't help myself when it comes to motivating others. Unfortunately, I forgot, in the past, to motivate myself!

I forgot to tell myself the same things I told others to help them move forward in their lives.

My Creator, the Lord God Almighty, had to take me on a journey that lasted a little over a year so I could get it. Get what? Get that I was a motivational speaker and author.

During those 13.5 months, He apprehended me and challenged me as I had (please get this!) never **allowed** myself to be apprehended and challenged before.

In my life, I had settled for the station in which I found myself. I had surrounded myself with folks who had also settled where they were. Now, these folks were waiting for me to get out of my comfort zone and the place where I had been for so long. During my exile, I allowed my Savior to apprehend and challenge me as never before.

He showed me how discontent I was in my supposed contentment. I wanted more but was content to settle for much, much less. I wanted to go on a quality vacation with my family but was content to complain about not being able to go on vacation. *What?*

Do you know how hard it is for me to write this for you to read? But, I also know that you need to read this and I need to write it so you can read it!

My past had dogged me so much that I thought I was able only to live in the way I had already lived. I didn't know that the Lord had determined something different for me.

But now I have been apprehended by my future! And, all I can tell you is, **WOW!!!**

My future is so bright, it's crazy!!!! As I allowed myself to be apprehended and challenged, doors began to open; doors that were not able to open before. Doors that I desired to walk through; doors I had allowed my past to keep closed. You see, I allowed them to remain closed because I would have been uncomfortable walking through them.

As I allowed my future to apprehend and challenge me, I began to apprehend and challenge my future.

I began walking through the doors! If I came to a door that was seemingly closed, I pushed it open and walked over the threshold. You can never imagine what happened as I crossed the threshold: *I was accepted*!

Not only was I accepted in most cases, I was fully embraced. You see, the people on the other side of the threshold had been waiting for me. Let's stay here for a moment.

In your future, there are some good things as well as some bad things awaiting you. I should say that the bad things only appear to be bad because you are apprehensive as you apprehend and challenge your future.

Let's look at the definition for apprehend: (1) Arrest, seize; (2) To become aware of; perceive; to anticipate especially with anxiety, dread, or fear; (3) To grasp with the understanding: recognize the meaning of. Understand, grasp.

My future arrested and seized me while I was in exile in New York. But at the same time, I became aware of and perceived my future. I also anticipated my future with anxiety, dread, and fear because I was comfortably stuck in my past.

Is any or all of this resonating with you? You see, although I was discontent with my past, I still wanted to stay there in my comfort zone. Although I greatly desired the future, my future life, I dreaded leaving the comfort of my mediocre past. I was so accustomed to it that I didn't want to apprehend my future or challenge it.

Many of you reading this book are stuck in the same place. I can empathize and sympathize with you. However, I will not enable you to stay there! I will encourage you to assess your current status and allow your future to not only apprehend you but challenge you as well.

Remember the lady with the couch at the beginning of this chapter? You are going to have to get rid of that old piece of furniture so you will have room for the new. You are going to have to clear out your closet so you can receive what is in your future.

Don't allow your past to apprehend and keep you in the place you don't want to be. As long as you keep those old things in your closet, they will clutter your life. Bag those things up in some of those heavy duty black plastic bags, take them to the dump and leave them there!

Do not live in your past. Do not focus on coulda, shoulda, woulda or gonna! Focus on what is and what will be as you allow yourself to be apprehended and challenged and you apprehend and challenge your future.

As you apprehend – arrest and seize – your future, it will also arrest and seize you as you become more aware of each other and become best friends. But, you will also challenge each other. Your future will challenge you to walk through the doors now open for you.

You, of course, will challenge your future to open up more and more doors for you more frequently. Your future will challenge you to go to greater heights and deeper depths of success than ever before. In turn, you will challenge your future to reveal those greater heights and deeper depths for you as you move with leaps and bounds toward even more rewarding success.

Someone is waiting for you to step forward into this new season in your life. They need to see you succeed so that they can step forward and be apprehended and challenged in their life.

Time is of the essence. Move forward as never before. Use your past for positive events to occur in your life. You don't have to live in the past allowing all the ugliness to embrace you. Instead, push the ugliness away (bag it up and take it to the dump!) and allow it to push you forward in the direction you need to go.

D.S.ofL. Let Go of the Past Key #2

My future apprehends and challenges me!

I apprehend and challenge my future!

This is not a one-sided relationship like you have had with your past.

As your future apprehends and challenges you, you must do likewise to it. Your future wants to be your closest confidante and friend. It wants to assist you in reaching your goals and dreams so you can have the life you desire.

Your future requires that you be truthful with it and yourself. If you are not truthful in your desires, you will find the relationship off and not as focused as it should be.

Push yourself to clean up your spiritual or mental closet so that your future can fill it with all your hopes, dreams, and desires surely coming your way in this season.

Chapter 3 - I'm Not What I'm Going To Be...

When you were a youngster and everyone asked what you wanted to be when you grew up, what did you tell them?

Doctor...

Lawyer...

Nurse...

Supreme Court Judge...

President of the United States...

I am almost certain that at every different season in your life, your answer changed. Your vision changed as you grew older and your view of the world around you broadened.

I remember at the age of 5 or 6 wanting to be a singer. I was influenced by the likes of Aretha Franklin and James Brown. Even now, I can hear the voices of my family laughing and their applause as I did the *Mashed Potatoes* and the James Brown split. I recall singing Aretha Franklin songs to whoever listened and people commenting on how talented I was.

That talent went with me to church as I sang lead sometimes with the youth and the adult choirs. I loved singing and my voice could be heard through the woods as I played or did whatever outside.

As I grew older, television shows like Perry Mason and Ironside caught my attention. My vision changed; I desired to become a lawyer. I held on to that vision for a good many years; even started working toward that. Unfortunately, it never came to fruition.

But what I really want you to see is this; even though you wanted to be all these different things, you weren't already...

Although you wanted to be a doctor when you grew up, you were not already a doctor. Sounds simple, doesn't it? But think about this; we oftentimes feel that we should be somewhere doing something entirely different than what we are doing right now. But we don't give ourselves time for preparation.

Becoming a doctor requires many years of general and specialized schooling. As a child, though, you may have been more interested in biology and science than the average student. As you progressed through primary and secondary schooling, that desire increased and you knew that you would become a doctor in your lifetime. But, you were not already...

You were not already... a lawyer. Although your favorite television shows may have been *Law and Order, Matlock, Perry Mason,* or *The Paper Chase,* you still had many years before actually taking the bar exam and sitting on your first case.

But, you always loved talking. You won the majority of the debates you participated in; even with your parents for the most part. You loved the high school debate team and won honors. When you graduated from high school, you knew that you would enter college with the intent of becoming an attorney. Then, after winning the admiration of your colleagues and superiors, you would be nominated to be a Supreme Court Judge, your highest desire. But, you were not already...

You were not already... President of the United States. But, you were a little politician. You had a name around your neighborhood (sometimes good, sometimes bad.) Honest (insert your first name.) You caused people (other children) to come together to fight for a united cause.

In high school, you ran for and won President of the Junior and Senior classes; you were a rock star in your own right. You never thought that you could **not** become President of Anything much less the United States. But, you were not already...

What I want you to see here, really tune in on is this; although you are not what you are eventually going to become, you can still become those things you want to become in life.

You see, many of us get off track from our greatest desires because of the curves life throws at us. We allow situations, circumstances, and people to throw us off because we lose faith that we can actually become what we desire.

When I was 16 years old, I became pregnant. It was 1975 in the South; South Carolina, that is. Upon discovering my condition, my family decided that I had ruined my life and would never be anything of significance. Their theory could not have been further from the truth.

But, I bought into it. I allowed myself to lose my vision of becoming an attorney because I was going to have a baby. *Surely my family was right and I would never be anything!*

Thank God that His vision of our lives is more solid and worthwhile than what others say about us. I didn't become an attorney but I did enter the military and served my country in various capacities for many years.

Now, in each of the professions I mentioned before – Doctor, Lawyer, Nurse, Supreme Court Judge, President of the United

States – I am sure there are stories behind each and every person who has gone on to become these things.

You see, in order for us to get to where we were ultimately created to be, we will more than likely have to go through something first.

Now, I will admit that it seems as though some folk's dreams occur at an astounding pace; of note, Susan Boyle and others who seem to come out of nowhere and achieve almost-instant superstardom. It seems as though they walk in it so quickly that others are not even able to compete.

But, just as it takes a certain amount of schooling to become a professional anything, your insides (your thoughts, emotions, and motivations) have to line up with whatever it is you wish to become so that when you get there, you will be well equipped.

I have met folks who went to law school, became an attorney and left the field after ten years. Why? They were dissatisfied! Some of them had been pushed in that direction by parents who lived vicariously through their child.

And then, I have met some attorneys who are still attorneys after 80 years. They love it; it is their life work! They will go to their graves with *Esquire* written into their epitaph.

That being said, what about you? Below, I have given you several questions to consider concerning your life. Ponder these questions; really ponder them. I have found that, in order to lead a passionate life, one in which I am purposefully and passionately fulfilling the destiny I was created for, I had to know my purpose.

Until I finally took up the full calling of speaker/author, I was impassionate but successfully helping others accomplish their destiny. I had given up on my dreams because of how I had been treated in the past and what others had told me.

It never ceases to amaze me the number of people who have worked in professions for many years but invariably do not know their purpose in life. Are you one of them? Have there been events in your past that have resurfaced, continually hindering you from making progress in fulfilling what you were created to accomplish in life?

Take a few moments and answer the following questions. Please don't write something quickly so you can continue reading the book; take the time to consider what you have always wanted in your life.

Probing Questions to Find Your Purpose/ Passion

1	What is it you really and truly want to do with your life?
2	What is it that, even if you never got paid one red cent, you would do just because it pleases you and you are really good at it?
3	What is it you have always wanted to do but your past has continually attempted to keep you away from?
4	Why haven't you followed your dream?

Many people stop hoping and dreaming when, at first, they do not capture their heart's desire. They stop because they feel that life is over and they will never accomplish their highest goal for themselves.

Our past can either hinder or catapult us into our future. Our past is something we have to go through first. Our past is the catalyst that will push us into our future... if we will allow it!

Just as in Chapter Two we found that we have to allow our future to apprehend and challenge us, we also have to apprehend our future and challenge it.

Philippians 3:12b, *but I follow after, if that I may apprehend that for which also I am apprehended of Christ Jesus...*

Although our future pursues us, it can also be quite elusive. The Apostle Paul, the writer of Philippians, gave us several clues as to the elusiveness of our future. He said in 12b, *but I follow after if that I may apprehend that for which I am apprehended of Christ Jesus.*

Now, by now, you know a little about my faith. Everything that I am, everything that I have been and everything that I am going to be is because of my faith in Jesus Christ. I have followed after Him and the apparent calling He has placed upon my life.

When I was in the military for all those years, I knew that there was something more to me than just being a soldier in all the different capacities I served.

As a private, E-1, I knew that I would eventually rise in rank to Private E-2, Private First Class or E-3, Specialist E-4 and finally Sergeant, E5. During this time, I did everything I could to become a Staff Sergeant, E-6. But, that rank remained elusive to me.

Even after becoming a Drill Sergeant, I thought I would score high enough on different boards to attain the rank of E-6; but, every time I came close, they raised the bar.

But, what if I stayed in the mindset that every time I approach a promotion, the bar is raised so I can't get promoted? You see, that's what causes many of us to falter; we look at what shoulda happened but didn't because of whatever reason. As we try again, we become disheartened because it seems as though we will never make it anywhere.

Then, because we perceive ourselves as stuck, we give up hope. Am I the only one this has happened to? As we contemplate the unfairness of life and how others seem to attain quicker and easier than we, we give up hope because we *know* that we will never make it to the next level.

But, I also want to warn you about something. Not everyone wants you to become what you know you were created to become. Some folks will do everything within their power to prevent you becoming what you where created to be. They don't want you to walk in the destiny you were created to walk in. Why?

There are many reasons but the two that readily come to mind are jealousy and envy. Look at Joseph's brothers in Genesis Chapters 37 – 50.

Joseph was the son of Jacob's old age; Jacob's old-age baby. Jacob loved Joseph very much because he was the son of Rachel, Jacob's first choice of brides.

Because Jacob loved Joseph very much, he spoiled him. He did for Joseph what he didn't do for his other sons. And the 10 elder sons did not like it one bit! As a matter of fact, after Joseph dreamed the dream placing him in a position of authority over his entire family, his brothers plotted to kill him. Eventually, though, they sold him into slavery.

The really interesting thing about this illustration is that Joseph went into captivity, away from his family, for 13 years. At the end of those 13 years, almost overnight, Joseph was placed in a position of authority ultimately saving his family from death through famine. You see, Almighty God does have a sense of humor: He had the last laugh over Joseph's brothers!

Although his brothers attempted to kill the dream, Joseph's Creator, Almighty God intended for that dream, Joseph's purpose, to come to full fruition.

There are many who want your dream to die as well. For years, they have probably prayed for your destruction and the destruction of your dream, your true purpose. You have tried everything to bring about the full manifestation of your dream, your purpose. At times, you have given up hope of ever realizing your dream.

You have been through really hard times. Debt, divorce, bankruptcy, death, failure and other trials have fallen upon you. Time and time again, you have decided to just throw in the towel only to have a spark rise up inside of you to try one more time.

The Drill Sergeant of Life says in this season of your life: *Don't Give Up! Don't Throw In The Towel! Don't Let Your Haters Cause You to Stop Doing What You Are Doing!*

You are a survivor! You know what's inside of you! You know that you are destined for greatness! This is your time! This is your season!

You are not already… But, you will be!

You see, upon becoming a slave in Egypt, Joseph could have stopped believing that he would ever be more than what he was. But, there was something inside of him, a certain level of greatness that presented itself at every turn. His master, Potiphar, saw this greatness, used it, and prospered.

Now, when accused of rape by Potiphar's wife (usually penalized with death,) Joseph was sent to prison for a crime he did not commit. He continued to prosper on behalf of the warden of the prison.

Think about it. Reflect on the various adverse situations you have found yourself in. Somehow, when all the chips were supposedly down in your life, you rose to the top as the star, didn't you? You have continued to prosper even though all the cards were stacked against you!

Again and again, someone has tried to knock you down and keep you at a place of inferiority so they could feel good about themselves. Time and time again, you have accepted these knocks and continued to make forward strides, even though the odds were against you. Although it may not seem like it, you never gave up!

In your heart of hearts, you realized you were far greater than what everyone else gave you credit for. You continued to hone your skills because of that **thing** inside of you. You continued to dream; albeit not as grand as the dreams you had in the past. But, you still had a dream. You were not already... But, you could be.

It's been a long, hard road. Many things have happened since your first vision. But your time has come. It's time to **let go of the past** that has hindered your becoming all you were created to be.

It's time to let go of the **P**eople, **P**laces, **P**ossibilities that were and concentrate on what is and what will be. Face it; your latter end is destined to be far greater than your beginning. All the stuff you have had to endure to get to where you are will be used as you push forward into your destiny, your purpose.

Motivate yourself as never before. Go back to the dreams you had, the visions that were given to you of the life in front of you. Let those dreams and visions push you over the ledge into the waterfall of success waiting for you.

You are not already... But, **you will be!**

REMINDER:

D.S.ofL. Let Go Of The Past Key #2

My future apprehends and challenges me!

I apprehend and challenge my future!

Remember: your future desires to be your closest ally and confidante. If you confide your deepest, most heart-felt hopes, dreams and desires to your future, your future will take those same hopes, dream and desires and run with them.

Your future is here for you. It has been designed to benefit you and your generations to come.

Don't let anyone or anything stand between you and the future you were created to have! Go forward and apprehend your future and challenge it!

Your future awaits!

Chapter 4 – But I'm Not What I Used To Be...

We, as a people, detest change. Especially change in the people with whom we have been comfortable. We hate it because we love the things in folks that give us something to talk about.

Now, you may wonder why I made the previous comments. Well, these are things I have found to be true.

As a teen growing up in SC, I did some things that gave me a very bad reputation. I hung out with the wrong crowd; had a teen pregnancy; cut school; got into drugs and alcohol; you get the picture. When I was younger, in other words, I gave folks much to talk about.

No one ever came to me to show me a better way. As a matter of fact, because of their inaction, my actions became worse and worse. I was very destructive toward myself and really didn't want to hear what anyone else had to say. Pregnancy didn't really slow me down; it only altered some of my actions.

As I grew older, many of my actions changed. I made sure I graduated from high school even though my guidance counselor tried to deter me as much as possible. I felt that graduating from high school was really important. I got a job but continued to live a destructive life.

The best decision I made was joining the Army. That one action in itself took me away from the atmosphere I had become accustomed to. Now, although my behavior improved, there were still many things in my life that should have been avoided.

But, I'm not what I used to be... By the time I hit 30, I was actually getting myself together. I slowed down considerably in everything I did. Around this time, I began reconnecting with many of the people I grew up with. Wonder of wonders, they didn't want to reconnect with me!

You see, I had, and here's that profane word I began this chapter with... *Changed!* No more was I that destructive little Stallworth girl.

By this time, I had been in the Army for about 12 years. I had made some rank and had a pretty good life. But my detractors, the same ones who had talked about me and dogged me as a child, were not happy about the change. They didn't have anything else to talk about me about! What a shame!!!

I had to weed through my associations and cut them off at the root. I finally found my true supporters and went on to reestablish relationships with them.

Now, after this occurred, I really began to look at my life. I considered how far I had come. Then, I realized that although I wasn't what I was eventually going to be, I definitely was not what I had been.

This morning when you woke up, you were not the same person you were when you went to bed last night. I don't know how it happened or when, but, sometime during the night, you changed. When you got out of bed, even before, your thoughts were different from the ones you had on yesterday.

As you woke up, you changed your mind about something you thought differently about yesterday.

Although you may have experienced the same dilemma, you didn't think about it the same way this morning. You are not what you used to be; even as of yesterday.

You see, we all constantly change. We will not be the same from day to day; we should honor this in ourselves. We need to embrace the new *'us'* every morning. We need to say to ourselves:

Today is a new day!

Today, I win!

Today, I beat the odds!

Today, I AM!

How did that feel when you proclaimed those things about yourself? Did it feel better because you knew those things to be true? Did it feel good because these sayings gave you hope? Really take a moment and think about how you felt saying those things.

Every morning when I wake up, the first thing I say is, *"Thank You, Lord, for another day! This is the day You have made; I shall rejoice and be glad in it!"*

I also acknowledge that I am one day and one step closer to the manifestation of the promise that my God and Saviour has made to me. You see, in affirming that this is a new day, the old day has passed out of my system.

Yes, yesterday, in and of itself, still exists. However, my deeds of yesterday, good and bad, are allowed to fade into the thoughts of yesterday. Now, the results of those good or bad deeds may be experienced in the days to come; but, I can't take them back. I can only move forward.

What I want you to understand, grasp, though, is the need to honor ourselves in the minute changes we constantly make in our lives. We are in such a hurry to criticize the bad things and criticize ourselves for what we did not do that we forget what we have already accomplished.

In Chapter Three, we learned that we are not already. We learned that in order to become what we desire to be in life, we are going to have to go through some things first. As we progress, we find that we are not what we used to be.

As children, we all did things we would later regret. Some of those things were public knowledge; many of those things, though, were private in nature.

Now, those things we did that were public knowledge are events we can actually redeem ourselves from, in and with. I thought that I was a horrible child growing up. I ran with a rough crew, teen mom, etc. But, as I shared earlier, upon connecting years later, many told me what a good person I was.

By the same token, the ones who didn't want anything to do with me because I had changed for the better? Well, their reaction to my change spoke volumes.

Now, those things I did behind so-called closed doors, created and presented skeletons I am still eradicating from my life. These are the things that more or less attempt to keep me locked in my past and prevent me from moving forward. These are thoughts and internal wars we all endure just to make it through to the next level of our lives.

I remember, especially during my teen years, having such conflicting thoughts the majority of the time. To be honest, up until a few short, maybe, ten years ago, I honestly did not believe any good would ever come from me. I never sought counseling or therapy which is the way of the world. As a matter of fact, I rarely talked about my deep feelings to anyone other than the Lord.

Now, I know therapists and psychologists have a purpose. But, I really didn't think they could help me. I knew me. I knew the wrong things I had done. I knew the thoughts I had thought against myself and others.

But, during this time I also learned the power of taking responsibility for ALL of my actions. That made a **huge** difference in my life.

As time progressed, I learned to lean more on the Lord and those He placed around me. I began letting go of the past so I could move forward. Now, I must tell you that this also is a work in progress. I continually lean on the Lord because He is much more capable than I am. He is much more able than I am and can handle more than I can.

You may have experienced, or may be experiencing, the same in your life. You may have done some things that are not common knowledge; only a few folks know about those things. But, I encourage you today to release yourself from those things!

You need to look at yourself with fresh eyes and see that, although some of the things were probably pretty bad, it's not as bad as you think. Allow yourself to move forward in the new you.

Speaking of the new you, think about this. When December 31 of any given year comes around, what's the main thing you think about? You see, many people create a list of resolutions to create an image of a New You for the New Year.

...Weight loss. ...Gym. ...Learn a new skill. ...Get a new position on current job or new job altogether.

They attempt to add a certain element of newness into their old life. Unfortunately, as they attempt to introduce these new elements, they tend to forget that they hold the old mindsets from the previous year: same eating habits, same gym habits or none at all, same everything. By the time March 1 rolls around, these poor folks are back at the '*you*' of last year.

Have you faced this yourself and wondered why you could never stick with the plan for a new you? Well, I hope this has helped you a bit. But, keep reading because the best is yet to come.

You must allow yourself to make forward strides so you can be all you were created to be. You were created to be, to do, and to have so much more than you have been, done, and had up until this particular point in your life.

You see, as our Creator, God did not put limitations on any of us. We are only limited by the limitations we place upon ourselves.

I learned early in life that just because someone told me I couldn't do something didn't mean I couldn't do what they said. I learned to look at things differently. I also learned to expand my parameters, my knowledge and my desires so I could achieve more in the face of opposition.

One major element I learned that can hinder one's progress or limit a person is the introduction of negative thoughts. A good friend of mine, Marcus Roberts of Daybreak Toast Masters, says, "*If you think you can, you can.*"

When he made this comment, it sounded so simple. But look at the opposite thought. "*If you think you can't, you can't.*"

Telling ourselves and others, "*You can't,*" starts a negative train of thought that dictates our actions from that point.

You see, once those words are said, our minds and the positive thoughts often cease.

You can't go to school because we don't have the money.

You can't start a business because you don't have the knowledge.

You can't get promoted because you don't have the skills.

It appears that '*can't*' and '*don't*' occupy the same space and time in our lives. But, look at the excuse compounded with '*can't*' and you will see that the '*can't*' can actually be a delay. Change the statement to a more positive statement.

You can't go to school because we don't have the money right now. But, if you get a part-time job, you can go to school and get your degree in Neurophysical Science!

You can't start a business because you don't have the knowledge right now at this very moment. But, if you take those classes and network with others of like mind, you can start that business and do very well indeed!

You can't get promoted because you don't have the skills right now. But, if you take the company-paid training and apply everything you learn, get a mentor within your field and push yourself forward, you will not only get that promotion, but also the next and the next as well!

Positive and negative thoughts and feelings are merely perceptions of what we want to occur in our lives. If we really want changes to occur, we must change our perceptions and realize that we create our reality.

When we notice that we have changed from just yesterday, we will also realize that every step we take, we change the scenery and the environment of our lives. We don't need to wait for an affirmation or a confirmation from anyone else. All we need to do is continue to make forward steps.

So, since I have given you the concept of forward steps, you must see that there is also the opposite – backward steps. Granted, we try not to take as many backward steps as we do forward. If we did, we would never get anywhere.

You see, you take backward steps when you hold on to the past and go back to those things that you should have already terminated in your life. What was said about you or done to you is no longer relevant in your life. If others continue to bring things back or remind you of what you used to do for whatever reason, you may need to remove those folks from your life.

Unfortunately, you can't remove yourself from your own life. But, you can remove those past thoughts, actions, and deeds from your heart and mind. Don't let those negatives keep you in a place that you don't want to be in.

By the way, one of the things that made me fall in love with the Lord is that He does not keep a record of any of those things. You see, once I repented and asked to be forgiven for all my past transgressions, I was forgiven. I was given free rein to move forward and do great things. You will find more about this in Phase II, Forgive, Forgive, Forgive.

So, just chew on this for a bit. Look at those past transgressions you committed and your past trials and tests. See that you are **NOT** what you used to be... You are better!

D.S.ofL. Let Go of the Past Key #3

I don't have it yet; but, I'm getting it!

Never believe that you have to get it right the first time... ***or else***! We will encounter very few activities in life that we will have to immediately succeed at.

From the time we begin walking, we find that, many times, we fall. However, when we fall, we don't just sit there and never get up until we are sure we can walk without falling. No, we get up and toddle around holding on to stationary objects until we can *get our legs under us.*

As we grow older, there are many other instances in which we *fall* but immediately get back up so we can continue.

Never give up! You may not have that ***thing*** yet... But, you're getting it!

Chapter 5 – Teaching Moments, Lessons Learned

I was recently reunited with a very close and dear friend. We had been together 20 years ago but lost contact for the last 17. In both our minds, our children were still the same. Unknowingly, I saw her son as the little boy he had been when I last saw him.

I remembered him so vividly! However, when I heard his voice on his message to incoming callers after all these years, I actually had tears in my eyes. *Where was my sweet, little Theoh?* He was a man; but I didn't want him to be a man!

One thing we must understand as we endeavor to let go of the past: others will try to keep us in the place where *They* are the most comfortable with us. They will attempt to hold on to *"the way we were."* They will actually fight you tooth and nail when you attempt to come out of their vision or view of you.

As I shared with you earlier in Chapter 4, many of the people I grew up with continually tried to keep me in the same mold they had grown comfortable with. They wanted me to be the same; but, for the life of me, I could not be the same person I had been. I had not made it to where I wanted to be. However, I was not going back to where they wanted me so they could remain comfortable with me.

Now, let's face it: the past is very comfortable and the future is exceptionally uncomfortable. In order for us to walk in the future, our destiny, we have to make ourselves very uncomfortable. And don't think that the past will not try to lure you back in. It will! It will dig up every device it can to pull you back in so that it will not lose one of its favorite participants.

When you finally determine to **Get Over Yourself and Let Go of the Past**, you will have to work harder than you have probably ever worked before. You see, not only will others try to keep you in the past, you will try to keep yourself in the past.

Let me give you a very simple illustration. Recently, I finally threw away an old, very old pair of tennis shoes. Those shoes were so broken in; it was like wearing a pair of slippers when I walked outside. But, I wanted some new tennis shoes. I have a pair of those expensive walking shoes but purchased the wrong size; I can only walk in them for so long.

As a matter of fact, I need to get rid of them as well so I can finally get my new tennis or walking shoes. You see, before I threw the very old pair away, every once in a while, I put them on and did my morning walk. Reaching for them was just a matter of habit.

There are habits holding you in your past that you need to release. It is very easy for you to reach for those People, Places, Possibilities And Situations (that should be) Terminated because they bring you comfort. They remind you of days gone by regardless of how unpleasant they were. But, you have to *want* to let go of your P³.A.S.T. in order to move forward.

Again, I warn you: You will manufacture reasons to remain in the P³.A.S.T. You will concoct and design paths of resistance allowing you to dwell in the P³.A.S.T., holding on to the *old you* while at the same time attempting to bring the new, improved you together with the old. Here is a very timely and appropriate verse of scripture for this dilemma.

Luke 5:36 – 39 *And He (Jesus) spake also a parable unto them; no man putteth a piece of a new garment upon an old; if otherwise, then both the new maketh a rent, and the piece that was taken out of the new agreeth not with the old. And no man putteth new wine into old bottles; else the new wine will burst the bottles, and be spilled, and the bottles shall perish. But new wine must be put into new bottles; and both are preserved. No man also having drunk old wine straightway desireth new; for he saith, The old is better.*

Why were those old tennis shoes so comfortable to me? Why do we try to wear out every stitch of a comfortable pair of Levis before we throw them away? And then, we cover as many holes as we can with patches until we can't add another patch!

Why do some folks, mostly older men, drive and maintain cars until the doors fall off the hinges? Or, they just run the car into the ground?

Besides the obvious, cars are just too expensive today. Most folks drive cars for years because it seems that the older they are, the better they are.

The same sentiment is found in Luke 5:36 – 39. The last line says it best: *The old is better.* But, that is not to say that our old way of life is better or our old stinking thoughts are better.

In order for us to move forward, and, unless our old ways provide everything we need to walk in the destiny that was purposed for us by God, we need to let go of that P³.A.S.T. We need to forget about those things which are behind and reach toward those things which are before us.

Also, another part of the illustrated scripture says that we can't put a new piece with an old piece. Unlike when we put a patch on an old, comfortable pair of jeans, we would not do the same with a classic suit. Now, I can't imagine this happening, but, if you were to wear a hole into the knee of a pair of dress pants, would you place a patch on those slacks?

I don't believe you would. Those same slacks would find their way to either the Goodwill bin or the garbage bin and you would make your way to JC Penney or Macy's to replace them.

Using the same scenario, why would you attempt to mix the old you in with the new you?/ Why would you attempt to hold on to the old stuff you used to do and mix it in with the new? Just doesn't make sense, does it?

It doesn't make sense because you are trying to go some place new and different in life. You are attempting to accomplish new goals and reach new heights so you can be all you were created to be.

We should all learn lessons from our P³.A.S.T. We should build on them so we don't run into the same People, Places, Possibilities and Situations (that need to be) Terminated in our future. If by chance we do, we should be well equipped to recognize them and put them in the place they need to be.

As you ***Get Over Yourself and Let Go of the P³.A.S.T.,*** you will find it is absolutely essential to drop some things in order to pick up others. Don't pour the new you into that old wineskin of life. You will burst through, leaving yourself naked!

REMINDER:

D.S.ofL. Let Go of the Past Key #3

I don't have it yet; but, I'm getting it!!!

Your future waits with anticipation and excitement!

Your future sees your daily struggles and knows that you are attempting something you never attempted before.

As you continue to move forward, bear in mind that the best is yet to come. Although you don't see the fruit of your labor at this very moment, you will!

You're getting it!

PHASE II
FORGIVE...
FORGIVE...
FORGIVE!!!

Chapter 6 - The Perpetrator

How long do you think one should hold another in their heart in a negative manner? Spiritually, we tend to do just that! Once someone has affronted us, we tend to hold that wrong in our hearts much longer than we should.

And the surprising thing about it is, we don't realize it! Sometimes, we don't realize it until we have created an immense amount of damage to ourselves and to the perpetrator.

The theme throughout this book is letting go of the past so you can grab hold of your future. I know, easier said than done, right? I've been in your shoes many, many times before. And, I'm almost certain you have been in my shoes many times as well.

When I was a child, I went through much that, over the years, I retained. I had no idea how to release or let go of my past. As a matter of fact, it sometimes felt darn good to retain my past because I had someone other than myself to blame for my failures.

54

Now, I guarantee that some of you reading this right now can identify (and probably agree) with me on that last statement. Here, let me say it again:

It sometimes felt darn good to retain my past because I had someone other than myself to blame for my failure!

You see, like many other people in our world today, many of us despise taking responsibility for our actions whether positive or negative. Sometimes, we actually hate having to *'fess up* to the things we have or have not done in our lives. We would much rather blame someone else so we don't look so bad.

Tell me, truthfully; have you been there? Have you been so caught up in your past that it actually felt better to stay in it than to come out of it?

Oh my goodness; that really hit a nerve with me just now!

Let me be the first to confess: I felt good remaining in my past and blaming others for my situation! I felt good wallowing in the mire of self-pity! Doing so caused me to remain comfortably ensconced in my past.

It felt good also to blame others for keeping me there. It felt good to throw my hands in the air and declare that I couldn't move forward because of what someone else had done to me or whatever to prevent me from moving forward.

Oh my goodness! What a bunch of malarkey!

Let's take care of this right now. Take a deep breath and repeat after me:

I AM NOT MY PAST!!!

Say it again with conviction:

I AM NOT MY PAST!!!

You see, what invariably happens is we lose track of our responsibility in the past areas of our lives because it feels better to our skin when we blame someone else for what we were responsible for doing.

Recently, I spoke at a Women's Conference. During the course of the conference, I admitted some things I had done when I was a teen. The things I admitted could have been prevented.

Now, at the time, and for many years afterward, I blamed unknown women for not talking to me and schooling me about the actions I took. These unknown women were my perceived perpetrators for that season of my life.

If they had given me advice, I would never have… I often said as I passed from one season to the next. But, the fact of the matter is I had a choice in allowing the things that happened to me; I could either say *'yes'* or *'no.'* The majority, of course, should have been *'no!'* Had I learned the power of *'no,'* many events could have been avoided or prevented.

But these were my choices. In most cases, no one forced the situations on me that occurred. There are always choices to be made. It is our decision and right to make either good or bad choices. However, we will also suffer the consequences of our choices.

It's like this: if you eat so much chocolate cake that you suffer a horrible stomach ache, whose fault is it? The person who baked the cake, the store for selling the ingredients, the person who concocted the recipe? Or, more simply, is it you? Did you make the choice to sit and eat as much of that cake as you possibly could? Or, did someone tantalize your taste buds forcing you to indulge?

The scenario above may seem silly but many people go back to the original creator of the delicacy so that none of the blame for their overindulgence is placed on them.

During the seasons of my life, I have learned to forgive my real and perceived perpetrators. I learned to forgive those I perceived as leading me down the bunny trail to destruction and distraction.

I had to forgive those who spoke badly about me and who never offered constructive criticism to me. To be honest, I don't even know if I would have accepted any constructive criticism anyway. I may have just continued on the road to self-destruction-ville to fulfill my thoughts of destruction.

The interesting thing about forgiving my real and perceived perpetrators is this: they didn't know that I held them in my heart in a negative manner. They had forgotten about the perceived situation and moved on. I discovered that this was an inside job that needed to be handled: inside of me, that is.

In forgiving my real and perceived perps, I was able to release them from my life in ways I never imagined: I was able to release them so I could release myself from all the blame, hurt and pain I continually heaped upon myself. I held onto those perpetrators in a very toxic manner.

Think about it: when you continually hold onto those who have hated on you for a very long time, you're not hurting them; you only hurt yourself. Just listen to your conversation concerning those folks.

I would have gotten somewhere by now if so-and-so had not done what he or she did to me.

I could have been an attorney if such-and-such had not happened to me.

I received my life because of so-and-so.

See how destructive these words and thoughts are? See how they pierce your very heart and soul? These are the kinds of words that destroy the mind and heart. These words make it difficult for the person to consider that there are more positive aspects of their lives they can build on and prosper in.

What if you turned it around and forgave those same perpetrators and... thanked them!

HOLD ON, DRILL SERGEANT! THANK THEM?!?!?!

Let me finish.

Yes, as crazy as it may sound, thank them. Thank them for giving you experiences that have helped and allowed you to grow in ways you never imagined. I know it's hard to conceive that you need to do this but hang in there with me for a moment.

You see, sometimes we have to do the unimaginable just so we can walk in the vision we have been created for. We really have to let go of the past so we can see our future. All the past experiences we have had are like cloud covers that keep us from seeing that the sun is actually shining all around us.

By the time I was 16 years old, I was pregnant. It's not that I was ignorant or slow in the true sense of the word; but, I was. I was looking for something – love, acceptance, me – in all the wrong places. I found other things that benefitted me in no way, shape, form or fashion.

People, mostly family, gave up on me. They told me that I had ruined my life and would never make anything of myself. They called me names, talked down to me and turned their backs on me. To which I say:

THANK GOD!!!

I know; you probably think I'm crazy. But consider this: if I had really bought into their theories of my life, I would have never tried as hard as I have in my life. Furthermore, I would have never succeeded in anything in life.

…And the baby that *ruined* my life? She is now 35 and a very successful businesswoman in her own right! She is awesome and very precious to me!

THANK GOD!!!

If I had kept or attempted to keep all those negative, naysaying folks in my life during all the seasons I have come through, they would have continued to drag me down into the vision **they** had for me. Worse, I would have fallen for it and accepted that this was all that was available for me!

THANK GOD!!!

I could have allowed my childish transgressions to hold me down. I could have had ten children out of wedlock, not have attained my high school diploma and not have served my country in the US Army.

THANK GOD!!!

So, yes, I say thank your perpetrators for everything they did to and for you; for everything they said to and about you.

Thank them for causing you to raise your head up, stick your chest out and throw your shoulders back in defiance of how they thought you would turn out!

Thank them for giving you a testimony because of all the struggles, all the heartache, all the pain you have been through.

And, you have been through a lot! But, you made it through! Let's just take a moment to celebrate.

Repeat after me:

I've had my struggles, but I made it through!

I've had very hard times, but I made it through!

I'm not what I'm going to be but I'm definitely not what I used to be!

I made it through and I'm going further than I've ever been before!

How does that make you feel? Take these affirmations, write them on sticky notes and place them in places you will constantly see them. Help yourself to see the new you.

Continually encourage you! Stop living in the past by constantly dredging up what *they* used to say. Do you even remember who *they* are? Do you remember their exact words? Can you recall your precise reaction at the moment *they* said what *they* said to you? Probably not.

Stop being a victim! Stop allowing those same voices from the past to keep you from moving forward because of some things you need to release from your life.

You see, our minds are crazy. One day, I was talking to our youngest son. He was telling me about something that had occurred when he was a child. I remember precisely the situation he spoke of. The only thing is, though, he perceived it in a way that was completely contrary to what actually happened.

The same happens with us now. The things we recall happening in our past are probably not the things that really happened. And if they are, guess what? It's in the past!

Your past does not define your present and your future; **YOU** do! Next to the Lord God Almighty, our Creator, *YOU* have the power to create your future the way you want it to be.

While in New York and the Lord was instructing me on how to present myself and what He wanted me to do when I returned to Colorado, I had a say in the matter. Either I chose to follow His instructions or I chose to follow the same non-productive path I had been on for so many years. I chose to follow the path He laid out for me.

And, I must say, His way is much better than mine. For example, in my previous season, it took me almost ten years to get one book out; and the book never really went anywhere. During that season, when I actually flowed in that gift, the second book of that season came forth in only three months. Of course, there were those in my life who said I wouldn't do well because I had no one backing me.

Fast forward to this season: I began writing the first book of this series, *How To Get over Yourself, Get Out of Your Own Way, and Get What YOU Want Out of Life!*, on March 16, 2011. I completed it on May 27, 2011 and released it on June 16, 2011. I think that's about 90 days all told, don't you? And guess what?

I am working on this book, the second of this series in, what, four months after the first was released?

You see, I can't consider the naysayers, unbelievers and Negative Neds of my past seasons. I have forgiven and released all of them because I am moving forward at an amazing pace. I can't harbor emotions and ill-thoughts against folks whose season has passed from my life. I have to be the bigger person. I must be the one to step up to the bat and say:

I forgive you. Thank you for giving this experience to me. I have grown from it. I release you from my heart and life. I hope that all goes well with you!

You are the bigger person. You can forgive the perpetrators from your past. You can thank them for the contributions they have made in your life. Now, grab hold of your future and move forward!

Remember in Chapter One we discussed how your future is pursuing and apprehending you, challenging you to become all that you were created to become in your life?

Forgiveness Challenge

1. Forgive the perpetrators from your past.
2. Thank them for all the negative and positive experiences they allowed you to have. Sit down and write a letter to each of them. In the letter, write about every situation you faced with them. Tell them how you grew out of that experience. Now, if you want, you could mail it to the person if you choose. I wouldn't. This is for you. After you write it, rant and cry over it, burn it and watch your past go up in ashes. Feel good about doing this.
3. Pursue your future.
4. Apprehend your future.
5. Challenge your future to take you to where you want to be in life.

In this chapter, we dealt with your real perpetrators. In Chapter Seven, let me show you some of your perceived perpetrators and how to deal with them and let them go.

D.S.ofL. Let Go of the Past Key #4

This *ONE* thing I do: I choose *TODAY* to Let Go of the Past!

Everything in your life begins with a choice.

When you awaken in the morning, the choice is yours whether you will have a good day or a bad day. Of course, others can come and attempt to change your good day into a bad day. But, you have the choice of whether you will allow them to be instrumental in ruining your day or not.

Letting go of your past begins with a choice. You either choose to let your past go and move forward into your future. Or, you choose to hold onto your past and allow your future to fade away into oblivion.

Choose TODAY to Let Go of Your Past!

Chapter 7 – Perceived Perpetrators

Let's talk about one of my favorite characters from the Bible: Joshua. After Moses, God's friend, stepped down from leadership, Joshua was appointed to lead the Israelites into the Promised Land.

Can you imagine leading hundreds of thousands of men, women, children and animals into parts unknown? You can also imagine, then, Joshua's thoughts when a man, obviously an other-worldly being, confronted him with a sword in his hand.

Joshua approached the man and asked, *"Are you for us or for our adversary?"*

And the man replied, *"Neither; but as the captain of the Lord's host do I now come to you."*

To the normal human, this probably would not have been a satisfactory answer. As a matter of fact, the normal human would have probably pulled a sword as well; you know, kind of even things up as much as possible, if you will.

Joshua was not your normal human in the biblical sense. Joshua followed, believed and had faith in the Lord God

Almighty. He had already followed the Lord while serving Moses. Now, he followed because he believed in what God was doing in the lives of the Israelites.

But Joshua could have perceived this being as someone against him. We all do the same thing.

When we experience someone coming against us because they don't agree with us, many times we say they are our enemy. We go to extremes in ascertaining that, if someone is not for us in every way, he or she is obviously against us.

Recently, it dawned on me that perceptions can hinder relationships. You see, the way we perceive something or someone may be completely different than the actuality. Let me give you an example.

Remember in the last chapter I shared with you how my son perceived something from childhood? Well, in this season, my son's habit is to start a conversation with me as though I have already been conversing with him on any given subject.

Not too long ago, I said to him, *"Son, just because you are having a conversation with me does not mean I know what you are talking about. When you see that I'm working, start the conversation at a place in which I will know what you are talking about. Do you understand?"*

Now, look at what he said that he understood.

"OK, Mom, you don't want me to talk to you when you're working."

HUH? That's not what I said at all. However, it's what my son understood. How? I have no idea!

I say that to say this; how many times have you perceived someone has done something to you just because of the way they acted or did not act concerning you? How many times have you mistaken indifference for persecution?

Not everyone will agree with you or you with them. Not everyone will act a certain way to appease you, nor you them. Those folks we sometimes perceive as being against us are merely following the path laid out for them! We can't change that; but, we can seek to understand them and allow them to understand us.

Those same folks you perceived as being against you may very well have been for you; they just didn't know how to present themselves to you because of the situation or circumstance you were already in.

You know, sometimes we get so down on ourselves, everyone looks like an enemy. If someone fails to smile at us or nod their head in our direction, we tend to think the person hates us. In reality, the person is merely passing, by lost in thought in his or her own world.

How many times has someone cut you off in traffic or zoomed into a parking space ahead of you and you spent the rest of your day in a funk? Did it ever occur to you that your perceived perpetrator went on his or her merry way without one thought of you at all? Did you ever consider that this is the way this perceived perpetrator operates? Probably not.

Now, put the shoe on the other foot. How many times have you unwittingly not smiled at someone or nodded your head in greeting because you were lost in thought? Do you realize that the person you unwittingly snubbed or ignored probably mulled over your unconscious action for the rest of his or her day? You may have ruined their day and never even knew it.

Sometimes, we are so caught up in self, we forget about others and how they feel about the same things we experience. We look for the bad guys but fail to look for the good guys; and they are out there! And it just so happens that **you** are one of the good guys.

Let those perceived perpetrators go from your heart! I encourage you to forgive these folks. Forgive them; not necessarily because they have done something to you but because you **thought** they did something to you. You have held them in your heart as perpetrators of evil long enough!

Forgive them because it feels good just to release another person from your heart; it frees up space in your heart so you can have some good relationships in there. Let me give you a classic example from, where else, the Bible.

Jonah was one of the minor prophets of the Bible. He was charged by Almighty God to go to Nineveh to preach repentance to the wicked Ninevites. Jonah **hated** the Ninevites! Those people had treated the Israelites very cruelly and Jonah wanted them to go to Hades and be done with it. He didn't want to save them at all.

So, the Bible reports, Jonah ran from that calling in his life. He decided to board a ship and sail away from the purpose for which the Lord had called him. But, the Lord God Almighty would not let Jonah off so easily. God put obstacles in Jonah's path to hinder his progress in fleeing what God had called him to do.

Jonah was very angry with God! He didn't want the Ninevites to change their ways so God could save them! He admitted that God was a gracious God, full of mercy, slow to anger and of great kindness. He knew that God didn't want to destroy Nineveh for their evil; but Jonah surely did!

We all have moments when we want all real and perceived perpetrators to be destroyed and removed from our lives. It doesn't matter to us whether these facts are real or perceived.

All that matters is that they have supposedly done us wrong and we want them to be dealt with.

Jonah felt the same for the people of Nineveh. He put all the Ninevites together in one pot, poured oil into the pot and prepared to light the match under the pot; men, women, children and all.

Misery loves company. When we are miserable because of perceived negative experiences in our lives, we tend to drag others right along with us!

Jonah was miserable! He reflected on all the cruelties of the Ninevites. Assigning himself as judge and jury, Jonah decided that none of the 120,000 inhabitants of Nineveh were worth saving. He would rather risk the wrath of God than allow a loving God to embrace Nineveh and save them from themselves.

We must forgive all the perpetrators in our lives; not for them, but for us. Unforgiveness is similar to cancer; it starts in the very depths of our hearts and eats at us from the inside out.

Unforgiveness causes us to die from the inside out because we hold onto perceived perpetrators in ways we should not.

Jonah was very bitter because of the persecution his nation had received from the Ninevites. This bitterness was a cancer inside his heart. It caused him to be disobedient to God and the calling God had on his life. Jonah walked away from loyalty to God because he held his bitterness and unforgiveness in a much higher position than he held God in his heart and mind.

Many times, the negative emotions we carry in our hearts towards others cause more damage than good. We must forgive! We must free these people from our hearts! If we do, our hearts will heal and allows us to move forward in life.

As you begin to free people, you also begin to feel better, lighter in your heart. As you release them, the clutter, bad thoughts and vibes you have harbored for way too long are thrown out as well.

When I graduated from high school in 1976, I didn't graduate from the hard feelings I had for those I perceived who *"did me wrong"* as I grew up. As a matter of fact, many times I caught myself rehearsing what I would do to them given half a chance.

I imagined meeting them again once I became rich and famous and ridiculing them in the same way they once ridiculed me. I wanted revenge! I wanted to get them back for every rotten thing they had ever done to me!

The more I thought about these folks, the bitterer I became in my heart. The bitterer in my heart, the harder it became for me to create and maintain viable, fruitful relationships with others. It was hard for me to really be friendly. Everyone was suspect to me! I didn't trust anyone and really didn't want much to do with anyone.

I had a very tight circle around me of those I allowed to get in. But, they only got from me what I wanted to give to them; nothing more. What a way to live!

I remember turning people away from me because I didn't want them to get too close. And, I certainly didn't want to get too close to them! Wow! Writing this is especially therapeutic to and for me!

I recall crying out for relationships that mattered in my 20s; relationships that were good. But, because of the bitterness and unforgiveness in my heart, I couldn't give the same to someone else. Time and time again, I ran into the same type people – takers – because I was a taker even though I didn't want to be a taker.

I couldn't have good relationships because I was not a good relationship!

I was an explosion waiting to happen. I didn't even know what a good relationship would look like because I had never seen one.

Can you identify with this? Can you see yourself in your past, even now, doing what I had done just so I wouldn't have good relationships in my life so I could blame everyone else?

Looking back and balancing my old self with my new, I now see how wrong I was! Others weren't the blame for the things going on in my life; not completely. I was! I was the one continuing to create negative situations and circumstances in my life. I did that so I could feel good about blaming someone else!

Now, don't get me wrong; there were real persecutions and real perpetrators in my life at the time. But, not as many as I let on!

In the beginning of my 30s, I really began to look at my life and assess where I had been, where I was, and where I wanted to go. In order for me to get to where I wanted to go, I found that I would have to let go of the past just so I could grab hold of my future. After I discovered this, it took me a full 20 years to do just that!

I began taking responsibility for everything happening in my life; good or bad. No longer could I blame anyone else for not being or having success in my life. It was all on me! Every hope, dream, and desire I had pushed back for so long was taken out of storage and reassessed.

"Hey, I'm not too old to accomplish this! There is still time!" I affirmed to myself.

I discovered that no one had the right to tell me I *couldn't* do something. All authority was in my hands to do what I wanted to do, when I wanted to do it, in the way I wanted to do it.

I released all the perceived perpetrators in my life and in my heart. I replaced them with hope, optimism, love for myself, and love for others. No longer was I bound by bitterness and unforgiveness; **I was free!!!**

What about you? Do you harbor bitterness and unforgiveness in your heart toward a perceived perpetrator? Do you need to release him or her and let go of your past? As you release these folks and any ill-feelings you may have, replace them with hope, optimism, love for yourself and love for others. Release them! Forgive them!

Isn't it time to dust off those hopes, dreams, and desires you have pushed back for so long? You know… the ones associated with these perceived perpetrators. They were pushed back because of what you thought they had done to or against you. Now is the time for you to begin dreaming again and to place more emphasis on moving forward in the new direction set before you.

Tell you what: take a deep breath. Let's cleanse some things out of our systems so we can move forward as never before.

INTENSE STRUCTURED BREATHING EXERCISE

Inhale – HOPE

My hope in the future is exceedingly bright.

I have hope for tomorrow that can in no way be diminished because this is a new day for me.

Exhale – Discouragement

I blow out all the bad winds of discouragement – thoughts and perceptions.

I am no longer discouraged.

Inhale – FAITH

I have faith in God.

I have faith in myself.

I have faith that I can accomplish anything I set my mind to.

Exhale – Doubt

Doubt is no longer a part of my physical or spiritual makeup.

I do not doubt myself.

I only have faith in what I do.

Now, doesn't that feel better? In order to move forward, sometimes we need to clear our hearts and minds during moments of stress, anger, hopelessness and frustration. We must clear our minds and hearts of all the negatives so we can take a step in the right direction.

Practice the above breathing exercise throughout the day. When practiced, these breathing exercises will enable you come to the place you desire to be.

REMINDER:

D.S.ofL. Let Go of the Past Key #4

This ONE thing I do: I choose TODAY to Let Go Of The Past!

You must choose to release your perpetrators, both perceived and real, from your heart. The longer you hold on to them, the longer it takes for you to grab hold of your future and move forward.

Your future is waiting for you to release those past experiences and grab hold of the new experiences it has for you.

Make your choice today to let go of your past!

Chapter 8 – Forgive God?

I know that many of you have already decided that I have flipped my wig judging by the title of this chapter. But, please, hear me out.

At one point in my life, I was so angry with God! I couldn't pray or praise or anything! I was past upset, past being miffed with my God. I was flat out upset with the God of my creation; the God of my salvation.

You see, God wasn't working as fast as *I* thought He should have been working on my behalf. Things were not working or happening the way *I* thought they should have been happening, either. I was just mad; MAD! Angry with God!

I never gave any consideration to Isaiah 55:8 – 9:

For My thoughts are not your thoughts, neither are your ways My ways, saith the Lord. For as the heavens are higher than the earth, so are My ways, higher than your ways and My thoughts than your thoughts.

When one considers the vastness of the God of the universe, one must also consider that His thoughts and ways are much higher, much greater than those He has created. I never considered this as I walked in silence, angry that He had not moved in the way I wanted Him to move.

I remember it being an all-consuming anger also. I remember going to bed at night, angry with the unseen God I had chosen to serve. I recall waking up even angrier because He hadn't moved for me during the night. I never considered that He was waiting for me to stop being angry and unreasonable so He *could* move in my life the way He desired to move.

One day during this stressful, hurtful season in my life, my pastor approached me. The first question she asked was, "*Why are you angry with God?*"

Of course, you know I denied my anger. First of all, how did she know? I hadn't said anything to anyone about the emotions I was experiencing. It was business as usual as far as I was concerned.

I got up every morning, went to work, came home. I was doing everything I had been doing. But, I wasn't really praying. I wasn't praising (absolutely NOT!) I figured that He had forsaken me because of some trivial thing I had or had not done.

But, I hadn't said anything about my feelings. Not even to Him!

As a matter of fact, I never even acknowledged Him during this period. To be honest, I don't think I really said two words to Him besides, "*Why?*" and, "*Why aren't YOU doing anything?*"

It never dawned on me that I was the problem. Or, maybe it did. But, like so many others, I glossed over that one fact.

So, I continued on my merry way until my pastor asked, "*Why are you angry with God?*"

Tears filled my eyes as I, first denied, then, openly admitted that I was indeed angry with God! She said the strangest thing to me.

"*You had better repent or you're going to die!*"

Now, many of you reading this book today would not have received this strong admonition. Many of you would have gotten your panties into a wad and flounced off spouting denials and fuming because of the unjust counsel of your pastor... and, of God.

There are also many of you who would say that this wasn't God because God is love and the God of love. Many of you would say that this just couldn't or wouldn't happen.

To each of these groups I say, continue reading! I promise you will find yourself in this book.

You see, I had to understand my walk with the Lord. He had already done so many things for me. The thing I was angry about was so small, so minute. In view of all He had already done for me, it was crazy that I would get angry with Him about the matter. I had to understand that He was working out this situation for my good and for His greater glory.

Let me interject something right here. I am not attempting to convert you to anything. I am a Christian; Bible-believing, faith-filled, Holy Ghost-filled, practicing Christian. This is my story. This is how I **Got Over Myself and Let Go Of My Past.**

You need to find your own path to enlightenment. This is the true path I have found and that found me. I have followed this path for over 20 years; it works for me.

You need to understand your walk with God. You must understand that all, ALL things are working together for your good and for God's glory to be revealed in your life.

I had to come to terms with the fact that, at times, in the spiritual and emotional sense, God will completely slay me. In other words, He would take destructive things out of my life and replace them with more meaningful things He had created for me.

I had to come to the realization that many things that looked good **to** me were not actually good **for** me. Even after slaying me, I had to trust Him. Remember Job?

In the Bible, there was a man by the name of Job. He was very wealthy and blessed with seven sons and three daughters. Well, the devil came along and wanted to test Job's faith. God allowed it.

In one day, Job lost all of his businesses plus all of his children. But, Job never became angry with God or said a word out of place.

In the next test, Job's body was consumed with boils. At this point, his wife came and told him to stop trusting God, die, and just get it over with. Job continued to trust God.

In retrospect, I see certain similarities between myself and Job. I can't really say I would have had the same faith and patience Job exhibited. All I know is that I am still standing and willing to trust God in spite of it all.

You must understand that, although God slays you, He still expects you to trust Him. Let me address the question you have roaming around in your brain right about now. God allows many things to happen in our lives just so we will grow and mature and be able to get through all the things we must endure. There is not some huge cosmic game going on in the universe to see what we are made of. God knows what we are made of!

He knows what we can endure and just how much of it we can endure. He allows us to go through these things so He can build us up and bring us to the next season in our lives. You must understand that, although you may have many afflictions, the Lord is able to deliver you out of them all; even if you are angry with Him!

Ask yourself today if you are angry with God, the world and everyone else just because things aren't going the way you planned. Ask yourself if you are mad with yourself. I know that this is a touchy subject! However, we need to touch this subject so you can make it through to the next season of your life.

After my pastor asked me why I was angry with God and I confessed, you're probably wondering what I did next. Well, I went home, got down on my face, and prayed.

You see, I discovered early in my walk with the Lord that there are knee-prayers; and then, there are full-body prayers. This was a time for a full-body prayer. I had brought shame to myself and to God. I had turned away from Him and backslidden in my heart, if you will. I sought total forgiveness from the Master.

I lay on the floor at His feet and wept. Oh, how I wept! And it felt good! I cried a good belly-cry! You know the type: when you finish, your belly hurts. My belly hurt but my soul felt good.

I repented for everything – every thought, every word, every turn I took away from Him. I repented for being so angry with Him that I couldn't even hear His voice. I repented for hating on Him and on my pastors.

You see, I really needed to let this go because, if not, I was not going to be able to move forward.

You need to do the same. You are in denial. You have been so angry with God that you can't even hear Him drawing you by

His spirit. You have been so angry for so long that the anger has become like a comfortable house robe and wrapped itself around you quite comfortably.

But, consider this: nothing is going to get better until you first admit and then submit everything! Admit the anger, the hurt, the pain, the confusion. Admit this to someone.

As Job went through his trials, three of his friends came and sat with him trying to make sense out of everything. They tried to get Job to admit to some wrong-doing; but there was nothing.

Job's friends tried to get him to admit that he had sinned against God in such a way to bring this judgment upon himself; but, there was nothing. Job and his friends were clueless as to the happenings in Jobs life.

Finally, Job opened up a little and admitted that he was confused. In his words, one can sense not only confusion but anger as well. Job was finally able to admit as well as submit this anger and confusion to God so he could move forward with his life.

Would it really be beneficial for you to admit and submit to the same? Absolutely! Trust me; it really works.

Then, after you repent, it's all right to say, *"Lord, I forgive you! I thought I knew what was best for my life. But, I didn't. Now, Lord, please forgive me!"*

And you know what? He will. He is waiting right now to be forgiven by you so He can forgive you. I know I am going to hear a lot about this. Many will come to me and say that this is blasphemous. But, I will say to you as the Bible says in Mark 11:25 – 26:

*And when ye stand praying, forgive, if ye have ought against **ANY**: that your Father also Which is in heaven may forgive you* *your trespasses. But if ye do not forgive, neither will your Father Which is in heaven forgive your trespasses.*

If you have something against anyone else, you need to forgive them. How many people do you know, right now, this very moment, which are angry with God? They may call it by many different names but a rose by any other name...

Forgive God! The things you are angry with Him about are minimal compared with what He has done, is doing, and will do with and in your life.

After Job repented, God replaced everything in Job's life. As a matter of fact, He practically doubled everything that was replaced.

Think about this: the only sin that leads to death is the one that has not been admitted, submitted and forgiven. Turn around; turn back to God and watch how quickly things will begin to happen in your life.

By the way, as soon as I forgave God, (I know; right?) repented and He forgave me, things began to happen. He turned everything around for my good and for His glory. I received favor as never before.

That favor is extended to the present time in my life. And, I have not taken *that* path of anger since!

Now, I know the Lord not only as Savior, but, also as Master, Redeemer, and, most importantly of all, Father. He is my Father, the One Who cares about me the most. When I'm not feeling well, I crawl up on His lap and He wraps His loving arms around me and comforts me.

When I am uncertain, He gives me certainty. Sometimes, I just crawl up on my Father's lap to watch a movie; He enjoys a good movie, too! I have learned to love on my Father in the same way He loves on me: continually and unconditionally.

King David is another of my favorite characters in the Bible. He was called and appointed by Almighty God to lead the Israelites. Now, David never got angry with God that I know about; but, he pushed buttons that brought God's anger upon him.

David committed adultery with a married woman and murdered her husband to cover up the result of their liaison. David did not repent until God sent a prophet to tell him of his sin. Although God was very angry with David, He didn't kill David as was the traditional judgment for adultery.

God forgave David. Now, don't get me wrong; there were repercussions for David's transgression. Suffice it to say, though, that God brought David back into fellowship with Himself. David went on to be one of the greatest kings of all time.

We must completely forgive God just as he completely forgives us. Now, some of you probably won't fully understand this. That's OK. Continue to read and, I promise, understanding will come to you.

I have walked this path for over 20 years now. Every day brings a new and deeper level of understanding. The more I walk it out, the more I understand. I truly hope that understanding comes more quickly for you and that you receive it more readily than I did.

D.S.ofL. Let Go of the Past Key #5

I am not my past. Therefore, I forget those things behind me and move forward in my destiny and purpose.

One of the main things you can accomplish to immediately spring yourself forward into your future is to forgive; yourself and others.

Forgiveness is the catalyst that will push you forward at an astonishing speed. Forgiveness is the one thing that will cause you to forget your past and move forward into your future.

Forgive… And allow yourself to be forgiven as well.

Chapter 9 – I Must Forgive... Me!

I now realize that there were many years in my life in which I did not love myself.

You see, I didn't feel that I deserved to be loved, by myself or by anyone else, for that matter. Yes, I had relationships; many relationships if that's what you want to call them. But, they were platonic at best; who knows what else at worst.

I was very standoffish in all my so-called relationships. I didn't expect anything, nor did I want anything other than what these entanglements usually offered: sexual gratification. My view of my life was skewed because of the way I had lived.

Now, mind you, I had made the choices that resulted in the way I lived. After many years, I realized I could have made better choices. Those choices would have resulted in a different way of life for me and those whose lives I touched.

When I entered the US Army in 1977, I became the female version of a wolf in more ways than one. Again, relationships were not high on my priority list. I merely existed. I didn't really care for the whole relationship thing anyway. I ran through men like running was going out of style. Let's face it; I was damaged goods and I knew it.

I rarely trusted people because I couldn't even trust… me. I knew what I was made of; trust me, it was not very good stock.

Now, I'm going to say some things in this chapter that will elicit emotions of pity and such. I'm not looking for pity, sympathy or anything like that. I'm over it; I wish you could have been around when… Well, maybe not.

Many years after the fact, I found out that I had been born to a divorced man and a married, geographically separated woman; two strikes even before I was born on the earth. I was born in 1959 in New York.

As years went by, I discovered the deceptions that had passed around me for me to be born on the earth. Sad beginning, huh? And that's only the beginning.

I was given away by my biological mother to my biological father who gave me to his parents. If I wasn't who I am, I would probably feel really unwanted right about now!

You see, my birth didn't do the trick for my mother to net my father; therefore, I had served my purpose. Enough said?

Growing up in South Carolina with my biological father's family is another story in itself. Suffice it to say that once my granddad passed away in 1973, there was no reason left for me to strive to be better than I was. My granddad loved me more than anyone I knew. And that love went with him to his grave.

After Daddy was gone, I needed to find another outlet for love. This began the most unsatisfactory journey of my life. OK, back to the Army.

As I said, I knew what I was made of. I didn't like myself at all. I was unsure of what I needed to do to change the dynamic in my life.

By the time I became a Drill Sergeant, I was completely disgusted with me. I mean, just how many mistakes can one make in life without finally imploding? I was a really good Drill Sergeant, an excellent soldier but my private life was... Well, you come up with a word and it was probably the right word at that season in my life.

I was so close to pushing the exterminate button on myself. I **hated** Beatrice; didn't like her one bit. I often wondered why she had lived for so long and with such a miserable existence.

Have you ever been just sick of you? So disgusted that you wondered how others even put up with you? If you have ever been this way, you can identify with my life.

Not for nothing, some of you may still feel this way. But, I encourage you, don't give up hope. There is one simple solution I finally discovered after many years of self-disgust and self-hatred. I had to forgive Beatrice.

I had to forgive myself for all the crappy things I had done or allowed to be done in my life. But it came with a price.

God stepped into my life. My closest friend at the time began asking really hard questions; questions that made me really uncomfortable in my own skin. Questions such as:

"Bea, if you were to die today or tomorrow, where would you go?"

"Have you considered Jesus?"

These questions required soul-searching to the very core. To be honest, I really didn't want to know the answers. I didn't want to hear about the final destination for people like me. Ignorance was bliss for me and I didn't want it any different.

But the way in which God the Creator dealt with me was truly amazing. He didn't send someone to me who had lived a righteous life from birth. He sent someone to me that had been just like me in more ways than one.

That meant more to me than anything!

You see, I would have scoffed at a goody two-shoes; I would have laughed the person all the way back to the altar of God. The Lord had to send someone who could identify with me; and, I with her. And it worked.

By the time He finished with me, I was able to make an educated decision on the course my life was to take. I was able to take a look at this Jesus Whom I had heard about for many years but never knew much about at all. I had heard various stories about Him but didn't know which story was the truth.

Long story short (I know you want to hear the whole story; come to my BootCamp!) I began to forgive people in and out of my life that I hadn't thought about for years. The molesters, the haters, the rapists, the gossips... I forgave them all. I could freely do this because I had been forgiven by Almighty God for all the crimes, sins, and transgressions I had committed against Him.

There was only one person I couldn't conceive of ever forgiving... *Beatrice.*

I tried to get around forgiving myself more than anything. I tried to love my neighbor even though I didn't come close to loving me. I found that I was more tolerant and forgiving of others who had harmed me in the past than I was of myself. There was nothing redeeming about me.

I was an awful, horrible person! I didn't believe I should be forgiven.

Yes, I realized that God had forgiven me. But I still busted my chops over the things I had done many years before.

Have you ever been there? Have you ever told yourself, "*I can never forgive myself for that?*"

Have you believed all those things others told you about yourself? Have you bought into their version of you, the one that doesn't deserve to live a joyful, fulfilling life? Well, I did.

I had done so many bad things in my life. I allowed these things to keep me from forgiving myself for a very long time. I believed that Christ died for me. I believed He was crucified for my sins. But, I didn't believe I should be forgiven; not by me, at least.

You see, *Beatrice* had become my arch nemesis in life. She was the enemy of enemies. She was a frienemy before I even knew there was such a creature. I hated her with all my heart because of all she had allowed me to go through.

I recalled the various situations she had caused me to be in. These situations damaged my self-esteem and lowered my self-worth in others eyes; more importantly, my own eyes. I recalled how she taught me to only allow immoral relationships with married men because I wouldn't get hurt as badly.

After all, I didn't deserve to be in a good relationship; I would only mess it up.

Beatrice had caused me to lie, cheat, steal; you name it, I did it. Most of the stuff I didn't even *want* to do; my dark side wanted me to do it.

Now, I know this may sound strange to many of you. But, do this the next time you need to make a decision: really listen to yourself. You will find that the two sides of you are at war with each other.

That's what I faced until I learned that there were two sides of me. I had to bring both sides of *Beatrice* into alignment.

As I cleared my heart and mind of those real and perceived persecutors in my life and forgave them every step of the way, Almighty God began dealing with me about forgiving… *Beatrice*.

I know… I know this sounds strange to some of you. But, think about this: who is your own worst critic? Who gets you into more trouble, real or perceived, than any other foe? Whose face do you see every time you look in the mirror? Yeah; I know. Go ahead and say it: "***ME!***"

I had to come to grips with bringing myself completely into alignment. The Bible speaks on this subject in James 1:6 – 8, *But let him ask in faith, nothing wavering, for he that wavereth is like a wave of the sea driven with the wind and tossed. For let not that man think that he shall receive anything of the Lord. A double-minded man is unstable in all his ways.*

I was unstable because I allowed my dark side to pull me to the dark side while the better part of me wanted to go to the light side.

And again in Romans 7:15, *For that which I do I allow not: for what I would, that do I not, but what I hate, that I do.*

You see, my life was a paradox. I was conflicted on every side. I was all over the place and needed to balance myself in all areas… if not, I would have hit the self-destruct button.

God, through Jesus Christ, brought me into alignment. He showed me how to forgive myself so I could move forward into the purposes for which I had been created. I forgave myself.

Was it immediate? No! As a matter of fact, on October 23, 2011, while working on a draft of this book, I had a complete and total breakthrough. While working on **this** chapter, I had to put the pen down and take a break as I considered where I could be if I would only forgive myself completely.

I had played at it for the past ten years or so. But on October 23, 2011, I finally, completely, forgave myself! Tears were shed; anguish cried out. When I finished, I felt the release within that told me I was finally done with my past!

Hallelujah!

I looked at me with fresh eyes, perhaps for the first time in my life. What I saw wasn't as bad as I thought. What I saw actually had redeeming qualities that could be brought to a place of goodness.

But back then, I began to love me. You see, I could not (and didn't) love my neighbors until I loved myself. I began to treat me better; and it felt good. I released myself from all the hell I had put myself through and then – and this is probably going to blow your mind – I *died* to myself.

That in itself has definitely been a process. On October 23, 2011, though, I died to the last bit of myself in that sense. I could see how I had sabotaged myself all these years because I was not completely dead to myself.

Now, I don't expect you to understand all of this but know this: until you can get all of you to line up with the true you that you were created to be, you will never fully realize your full and complete potential.

Look at some of the more successful folks around you. Do you see how they single-mindedly go for what they want in life? Do you see how they do not struggle with that part of themselves?

You see, these folks are in control of every thought, every action they take because they have brought self in line. You can do the same. How?

The Drill Sergeant of Life says, *Repeat after me:*

I am who I have been created to be.

I single-mindedly do everything I need to do to get to where I want to be in life.

I am not double-minded.

I am not conflicted.

I am single-minded and I am going into my divine destiny with purpose and resolve.

How does that feel? I encourage you today to go back through the annals of time and forgive yourself for every incident that was contrary to the way you wanted to live. Once you do this, you will be pleasantly surprised to see the changes that will take place almost overnight.

You will not be sorry for forgiving yourself. You will be able to love you and those you come into contact with more deeply than ever before.

OK, now that we are over half-way to completion, let's review the **Let Go Of The Past Keys** we have so far:

Key #1 – I'm not perfect but I'm willing.

Key #2 – My future apprehends and challenges me! I apprehend and challenge my future.

Key #3 – I don't have it yet; but I'm getting it.

Key #4 – This ONE thing I do; I choose TODAY to Let Go of the Past.

Key #5 - I am not my past. Therefore, I forget those things behind me and move forward in my destiny and purpose.

Chapter 10 – Spiritual Cleansing

Now that you have forgiven everyone you need to forgive – the true and perceived perpetrators in your life, God, and yourself – it's time to move on. It's time for a deep spiritual cleansing to remove all the filth, all the sludge of the past.

Personally, I go to the scriptures, the Book of Books, for spiritual cleansing. In Psalm 51, King David poured out his heart to His Creator, Almighty God.

David was much like us; he committed crimes against God and humanity causing him to feel empty and filthy on the inside. Empty because he had become void of emotion, void of the need to do what was right in his own mind. Filthy because once he realized the temerity of his actions, he saw how ugly he had been. This caused him to be filthy in the eyes of the Lord.

But, I digress. Let's back up. You see, King David was chosen by Almighty God to lead the nation of Israel. A little shepherd boy, the youngest of his father's sons, David was a giant in the eyes of God.

While just a boy, not only did he kill a lion and a bear who threatened his father's sheep, David also defeated the giant

Goliath who threatened the Army of God. David did not allow obstacles to come between him and doing what was right by God.

Then, along came Bathsheeba. I talked a little about King David in Chapter 8; in this chapter, let me tell you a bit more about him and Bathsheeba.

From all accounts, Bathsheeba was a beautiful young woman; she was also someone else's wife. Her husband, Uriah, fought in the Army of Israel, the Army led by King David.

One night, while his Army was in the field and King David was in the rear at his royal palace, the King could not sleep. Walking on the roof of the palace, he happened to glance across the way and spied Bathsheeba taking a bath. By rights, David should have gone back to bed and called for one of his many wives.

Unfortunately, he didn't; he called for someone else's wife.

Now, an affair was one thing; murder was something entirely different. As a result of the consummation of David's lust, Bathsheeba became pregnant. David attempted to cover his indiscretion by calling Uriah in from battle. The king hoped that Uriah would come home and sleep with his wife.

But, Uriah was more honorable than the king; his fellow soldiers could not sleep with their wives, neither would he.

So David put a contract on Uriah. He conveniently had him killed in the heat of battle. Problem solved? Well, not quite. God saw all that happened and He called David on it.

Now, don't think that this happened overnight; David didn't immediately repent. Bathsheeba was pregnant, her first husband was dead and life was lived. God had to send his prophet, Nathan, to tell David a story that pricked his conscience. It worked and David repented.

Now, David was a Psalmist; he wrote the majority of the book of Psalms, poems of his journey with and feelings for God.

One Psalm in particular was written for the occasion of David's transgression with Bathsheeba. Psalm 51 is the cleansing poem David wrote to the God of his salvation. Verses 2, 7, and 10 are cleansing scriptures David used to bring himself back into fellowship with the Lord God Almighty.

2. Wash me thoroughly from mine iniquity, and cleanse me from my sin.

7. Purge me with hyssop and I shall be clean: wash me, and I shall be whiter than snow.

10. Create in me a clean heart, O God; and renew a right spirit within me.

There will come a time in all our lives when we will have to spiritually cleanse ourselves. Unlike in the physical or natural when we take a soap product, a wash cloth or buff puff, and step into the bath or shower, spiritual cleansing can be much more intense.

Spiritual cleansing means that you empty out the very essence of your being until you become void of everything that could possibly sully your inner being. Spiritual cleansing means opening yourself, in my case, to Almighty God and asking Him to thoroughly cleanse me according to His Word.

You see, the Word of God is like water flowing from a source like no other. When that water comes to me, it cleanses every thought, every motive, every emotion that is contrary to what God has for me. I take the Word, read it, and allow it to shower away the filth and other stuff that has cropped up in my life.

Wash me thoroughly from mine iniquity and cleanse me from my sin...

When I first received Jesus as personal Savior, I wept before Him as I had never wept before. And as I wept, everything that needed to come out came out with those tears. The hurt, the frustration, the pain, the private and public sins I had committed; everything. And it felt soooooo good!

His Word thoroughly washed me! It went into all the crevices and corners of my life and pulled everything out that needed to be pulled out. The Word of God went in and cleansed me from all my sin and iniquity.

By the time He was finished with me (and it is an ongoing process,) spiritually, I was as light as a feather. I felt refreshed, renewed, and relieved. I had a new lease on life!

Now, I can only share my experience with you. I don't know how people from other backgrounds do this. I only know what I have learned in my life. It's just like taking a shower. Not only do you take a shower to cleanse your skin, you take a shower to feel refreshed.

Spiritual cleansing is important in our lives so that we will always feel refreshed and ready to embark on the next challenge of life. The obvious second step David took in his cleansing process was to ask God to do something drastic for him.

Purge me with hyssop and I shall be clean; wash me and I shall be whiter than snow.

Purge means to clean of guilt; to free from moral or ceremonial defilement.

Hyssop – a plant used in purificatory sprinkling rites by the ancient Hebrews.

The Hebrew or Israelite people were serious about cleansing. They participated in periodic cleansing ceremonies to keep themselves clean before God.

David requested that God clear him from all his guilt and free him from moral or ceremonial defilement. He seriously wanted to come back into right standing with God and all God had called him to and appointed him for.

David desired to be sprinkled with the water of the Word of God so he could get back to his purpose.

I like what Jesus said to a group He called hypocrites in Matthew 23:25 – 28:

25. Woe unto you, scribes and Pharisees, hypocrites! For ye make clean the outside of the cup and of the platter, but within they are full of extortion and excess.

26. Thou blind Pharisee, cleanse first that which is within the cup and platter, that the outside of them may be clean also.

27. Woe unto you, scribes and pharisees, hypocrites! For ye are like unto whited sepulchers, which indeed appear beautiful outward, but are within full of dead men's bones, and of all uncleanness.

28. Even so ye also outwardly appear righteous unto men, but within ye are full of hypocrisy and iniquity.

If our *inner* man is full of anxiety and turmoil, fear and frustration, those things eventually make an appearance through our **outer** man. We must seek spiritual cleansing so we can be whole – spirit, soul, and body. We must make the effort to get our mind single so we can move forward into our divine purpose and destiny.

In this phase of **Get Over Yourself and Let Go of the Past,** we have dealt with forgiveness: forgiveness of others, forgiveness of God, and forgiveness of self. If we do not forgive others, we will never be able to seek forgiveness for ourselves nor forgive ourselves.

The last step David took to be completely cleansed was to ask God to...

Create in me a clean heart, O God; and renew a right spirit within me.

What does your heart look like right now? I know you can't take a gander at that organ inside of your chest cavity without the aid of electronic medical equipment; but, look at your spiritual heart. What does it look like?

Do you have anger in your heart because of things someone did to you in the past? Do you have and hold hurt feelings you feel you may never get over? Do you have anger against yourself? Do you feel that you will always carry these feelings because what you did was so horrible?

Now, you need to understand that you can fake good feelings. You can have complete chaos on the inside; but, if you have mastered emotional camouflage techniques, very few people will know. Very few will know how much you hurt and how angry you truly are.

But, by the same token, you will not make many great strides forward because you harbor these negative emotions and feelings.

I have given you a multitude of methods to not only forgive others and yourself but also to cleanse yourself so you can go forth and do the great things you were created to do.

In closing Phase II, **Forgive, Forgive, Forgive**, I challenge you to make a promise to yourself today; actually two promises.

1. *I will forgive others, God and myself.*

2. *I will seek cleansing so I can be whole.*

Love yourself as never before. Do unto yourself the same as you do to others. Become single-minded in everything you do. Embrace the change coming into your life. ***Get over yourself and let go of the past!***

REMINDER:

D.S.ofL. Let Go of the Past Key #5

I am not my past. Therefore, I forget those things behind me and move forward in my destiny and purpose.

My destiny and future are much more important than my past. As I let go of the past that has hurt me and through which I have hurt myself and others, I choose to grab hold of my future which has only good things for me.

I am not my past. I am not the hurts and pain. I have good things in store for me and I am going to get those things.

I move forward into my destiny with purpose and resolve!

PHASE III

FORWARD!!!
MARCH!!!

Chapter 11 – Change Your Focal Point

I want you to take a moment and do something for yourself.

In the spirit or in your mind, slowly do a complete 360° turn. While turning, look at all you have been through. Now, come full circle to where you are right now. This may take a bit. In completing this 360° turn in your mind's eye, you see every season of your life.

In some of those seasons, you may experience some emotions you had forgotten about. Some will be positively painful. Some, you won't be able to bear. If you must, pass through those seasons and come back to them when they are a little more bearable.

Currently, I am 52 years old. I have 50 years of memories I can go through and catalog. For the first 13 years of my life, there are mostly good memories. I recall the ages of two and five very vividly; I accidentally burned myself on a wood stove, on the thigh at two and on my neck when I fell on the stove at five.

Now, those particular memories may be painful in nature but I remember the love surrounding me during those devastating episodes. I am able to change my focal point from the bad to the good. Does that make sense?

At the age of nine, I recall Daddy teaching me to drive his old blue and white Mercury. I was tall for my age. He let me drive when he went to the houses of some of the people who worked at the textile mill. At their homes (now, remember, this is before the age of garbage disposals,) we picked up the pails of slop (leftover food) they gave to Daddy for our hogs.

When Daddy slaughtered hogs every autumn, these folks came and were gifted with portions of the meat. Those were good times!

Then, Daddy died when I was 13, one of the most traumatic episodes in my life. Because I was not allowed to visit Daddy in the hospital before he died, I was very angry. I wasn't able to tell him that I loved him. This was a very painful time so I may have to come back later so I can change my focal point on that event.

Now, what do you see as you slowly do your 360 through your life? Do you see all your past mistakes, foibles, and transgressions?

But, do you also see your successes? Your good times? Your happy days?

I can see age 14 when I was selected for JV basketball! *What a feeling that was!* And I was good! Mind you, I still hurt because Daddy was gone; but, I was able to focus on basketball and allow good things to flow again.

You see, in that 360° turn, you experience everything you have ever done: good and bad. That's good. Now, how do you feel? What are you thinking as you complete the circuit of your life in your mind? More than likely, you are experiencing mixed emotions right now.

Why did I do that?

What was I thinking?

How in the world did I get myself in that predicament? **What was I thinking?**

Unfortunately, we tend to focus on all the bad stuff that has happened in our lives. I know; it's natural. As people, we look more on the negative than the positive. As we grow older, we become more jaded and completely forget what positive looks like!

OK. Now, this is what I want you to do. Go back to the event which caused you to say,

Why did I do that? What was I thinking?

Does the moment have any redeeming points or qualities? While tossing those thoughts around, check your attitude during this situation. Were you positive or negative about the situation? Nine times out of ten, you were negative because it evoked the thought,

What was I thinking?

Now, as you went through the event, did you think of ways to correct or enhance the outcome of the situation? Or, did you just muddle through, expecting a negative end… which you received?

What I recently discovered, and it's probably been this way all along, is that I never really expected a positive outcome as I went through these situations. As a matter of fact, when something positive happened, I was really quite surprised.

We need to change our mindset! Surprisingly, it takes less energy to expect a positive outcome than it does a negative.

Check this out: when you expect a positive outcome, your body relaxes because you sense the eventuality of what you truly desire to come to pass or manifest in your life. You relax as you imagine the good that will come. Your body reacts to the relief it experiences because your desire is finally here.

But, in expectation of a negative outcome, your body tenses. It prepares itself for the disappointment of yet another failure. You speak defeat to yourself and run the gamut of emotions that failure brings on. You don't expect anything but the worst and that's what you get.

Look at all the energy you wasted with that negative emotion!

The next time you expect something to happen, take the bull by the horns and expect a positive result. Don't allow the situation or circumstance surrounding the event to dictate how you react. Take control of the matter and watch the positives that result from your actions.

You see, a good friend and fellow Army veteran, Doug Nichols, made a very profound statement during our conversation not too long ago; I won't soon forget what he said. He said to me,

Bea, I'm getting what I'm getting because I'm doing what I'm doing!

Take a moment to think about this statement...

You're getting what you're getting because you're doing what you're doing!

Go back into the annals of your mind. You will find that every outcome you experienced for every situation you went through came about because of what you were doing at that particular time in your life.

Say WHAT!!!!

Everything you have ever accomplished, positive or negative, was because of what you were doing at the time! If you really think about it, though, it makes sense.

You're getting what you're getting because you're doing what you're doing!

Now, the title of this chapter is, *Change Your Focal Point.* For a long time now, you have probably looked at your past as the most negative season of your life. More than likely, you have viewed it as a key element in your inability to move forward.

But, please, for yourself, change your view of the situations you have encountered. Change your focal point of the experiences you have endured up until this point.

Let's go back again one last time and turn 360° in our minds, our spirits. Let's look objectively at everything that has occurred in our lives as far back as we can remember.

Now, pick a spot in your history. You see, we are going to change your focal point. We are going to move forward from your past so we can accomplish some really good stuff in your future.

OK. Do you have your point? Now, is it good or bad? To be honest, it doesn't really matter. This is your event; this is your experience. Whatever you see, we can change it.

In my previous book, *How to Get Over Yourself, Get Out of Your Own Way, and Get What YOU Want Out of Life!,* we discussed Abraham, the father of Israel. He had a practice that I frequently use; it comes from Romans 4:17;

...and calleth those things which be not as though they were.

We are going to change the dynamic for whatever period in your life you stopped at. We are going to call those things that are not as though they are.

OK? Now, look at the situation you focused on. Can you see past that particular experience? I know; you have already seen the bad side of it; but, do this. For every bad you see in that situation, show the good side to yourself. I know it seems a bit strange, but, try it. Let me give you an example from my life.

In no way do I advocate teen pregnancy. As a matter of fact, I believe that abstinence is the best way and that young people should wait for marriage. When I was 16, I became pregnant. At the time, in the South where I was raised, I was told that I had made the biggest mistake in my life and I would never get anywhere in life.

My high school guidance counselor informed me that I would have to quit school because I would never be able to raise a child and finish high school.

Now, back then, I had no idea about what I am writing about today. But, I knew how to change my dynamic. I could have quit school, gone on welfare, and had my baby; probably eight more besides. But, that was not the picture I had painted for my life (especially with all those kids!)

I rebelled against the so-called authority of my guidance counselor; I graduated from High School. I went on welfare for a short, very, very short time; I did not like the way it made me feel. Instead of having more children, though, I chose to enlist in the US Army and get away from the environment encouraging my behavior.

During this time, I lost contact with many of the people I had hung out with; people who neither encouraged nor discouraged my actions. These people were just there to ride the highways of life with me. Losing contact with them was probably one of the best things to happen.

You see, now that I was out of that environment and in the Army, I made better choices in the people I connected with. The Army proved to be a more disciplined, structured environment for me. Don't get me wrong; I still made bad choices. But, now I was in charge. I learned to say '*No*' more often and '*Yes*' only when I **really** wanted to.

To some of you, this may not be a very good example. For me, it has served me best of all when I chose to look at my past and judge where I am going in my future.

Your experience might be:

Job loss - Bad side.

You now have more time to find the true purpose for which you were created – Good side.

Your supposedly best friend turned his or her back on you – Bad side.

Now you can assess the relationship and see that it was mainly one-sided; yours – Good side.

You see, we have the ability and the authority to change every negative event into something more conducive to our moving forward.

OK, let's go one step further then. I want you to practice what we have done so far.

Look at your present life, whatever point you are right now. Are you walking in the purpose you were created for? (Because of the importance of finding your purpose, I have included a copy of my *Drill Sergeant of Life Find Your Purpose Questionnaire* ® from my first book in Appendix A.)

Now, whether you are walking in your purpose or not, look at everything going on in your life. Is everything favorable for you? …Unfavorable? …Mediocre?

What are some of the things you can do to change the dynamics? How can you cause everything to line up with the direction you are headed? Here is one method I have found helpful in changing the dynamics in my life.

Using the *File Cabinet of Life* ® in Appendix B, start in the center by noting your current age. **[I would suggest that you copy this graph and enlarge it.]** In each square from the center, write every five or ten years going all the way back to zero. I am 52 and chose to start with 55 since I will be 53 in less than six months. If you are 32, you may choose to write 27, 22, and so on until reaching zero (0).

The *File Cabinet of Life* ® is a tool to help you recall and annotate the significant events in your life. Each bold line represents five (5) or ten (10) year increments from zero until your present age. One of my associates informed me that this graph is like a mountain; you climb from zero (0) until the present. Bear in mind that some of the passages are more difficult than others.

In the spaces between the lines, open the *File Cabinet* to the events you remember. In doing so, you pull those things out that might keep you from moving forward into your purpose and passion. When you pull these things out, you either fix them or throw them into the *Round File of Life* ®.

Beginning at zero (0), make a dot and draw a line from the bar at the age of your first cognitive memory; do this in the space to the left of the number. You can also take additional paper and write your memory.

My first cognitive memory was at two when I burned my thigh on the wooden stove in the house I grew up in.

Continue to dot and draw lines at each age where you have a *significant* memory. Once you reach the center or now box, put the sheet aside. Think about all the memories you dredged up. Some of these memories are good; some are bad.

Some memories are so bad you really do not want to drag them up. Hang in there! At this point, you may choose to allow the graph to sit for a few days. By the same token, you may decide to soldier on.

Take up the graph again. On the opposite side of the number, annotate the emotions, feelings you experienced when you went through each of the events you listed.

When I was two and burned my thigh on that wooden stove, I distinctly remember the love from my family that surrounded me.

"Awwwww. What happened to that baby?!?!"

"It's alright, honey! It's gonna be alright!"

Even though I didn't recognize it as such, I remember the concern of my family as each of them comforted me and tended to my burns. I felt that love and remember it to this day.

At five, when I fell on the stove and burned my neck, I remember being cradled in Daddy's arms and crying as he comforted me. I remember feeling shocked that I fell on the stove. Daddy rushed to pull me off the stove! As he did, I remember smelling my flesh as it burned.

Again, though, I felt the love and caring from my family.

As you go through, reliving the emotions of those past events, also do a series of mental $360°$ turns so you can get the full picture of the memory. Don't be surprised when these memories evoke strong reactions; we are going deep into your memory so we can make changes that need to be made.

Now, choose a memory. Unfortunately, for progress sake, it will probably be one of those that you really don't want to relive. For discussion sake, I will choose age 16 when I had my daughter, Tara.

This was a very discouraging time in my life. The same family members who loved me the two times I burned myself on the woodstove now turned away from me. They chose to believe I was a bad seed and vehemently told me I had ruined my life. They effectually told me that nothing good would come out of my situation and I would never be anything in life.

But this is my life and I choose to change the dynamic!

Now, remember; Abraham called those things that were not as though they were. I choose to remember the birth of my child as a time of joy rather than disgust or heartache.

I choose to remember the triumph of graduating as a single mom and the opportunities I created for myself rather than the looks of pity and the doubts I faced from others as I moved forward in life.

I decided to change my focal point so I could have peace in my life. I knew there was hope for me as I moved forward toward the various successes ahead of me.

Change your focal point! Don't look at the bad and decide it's going to stay that way because you can't do anything about it!

You're getting what you're getting because you're doing what you're doing!

Change what you are doing! Get more aggressive in your actions! Move from passivity to action concerning your life. It may take a bit but watch how your life changes as you aggressively (not passively) go about life with a focal point of positive successes.

If you are passive, nothing will change. Change your focal point!

As you fill in the graph, courageously step forward in the direction you want to go. Don't allow your past to draw you back in.

Remember, your past is your comfort zone. It will always give you a warm and fuzzy as it attempts to hold you captive. Your future is uncomfortable; as well it should be.

As you pursue your future, you will find that you will become comfortable with it to a certain extent. But remember, every day that passes is your past. You must not try to relive each day but forge ahead so your future remains fresh.

D.S.ofL. Let Go of the Past Key #6

I have the power to change the outcomes in my life!

Almighty God is the Captain of my soul. He has given me the authority to change my life and to make it into what I want it to be.

I am not powerless in my quest to be all that I have been created to be. I am not clueless as to the direction I need to go to make it to the top of my game.

I am powerful and have the wisdom and drive I need to go where I want to go and get what I want out of life!

Chapter 12 – Resist Revisiting

After beginning the process of cleaning out your ***File Cabinet of Life*** ® in Chapter Eleven, how do you feel? What thoughts or questions do you have that need to be answered before we proceed? Write them down and take a moment to really think about the direction you are going.

1.

2.

3.

4.

5.

Now that you have broadened your thinking and changed your focal point, it is important to go back in and close the doors of the areas you no longer need to visit. Some areas in your life need to remain in the past. It is crucial that you let go of these areas for they will hinder your progress the most.

Think of it this way; a person who has been an alcoholic is actually still an alcoholic in the truest sense of the word. If that person continually revisits his or her old haunts, eventually he or she will return to their old ways. Why? This is a comfortable place for them.

Gambling, drugging, drinking, stealing – these places need to be avoided if one is to successfully progress.

You need to resist the urge to revisit those old things and turn toward the new in front of you.

Let me ask you something. When you move out of a house or apartment, are you able to go back and revisit that place as though you still live there? Can you hold on to the keys and come and go as though you still have ownership of that old dwelling place?

I don't believe so. You have to leave it so that the new occupants can take ownership and authority of that place.

Another great challenge you will face in letting go of the past will be the people you used to hang out and do things with. Those folks, some well-meaning and some not, will attempt to draw you back into the way you were. But, what do you want? What are your desires for your life?

We have come a long way since beginning this journey of getting over self and letting go of the past. Even as of the last page you read, you have changed yet once again. Although you would feel comfortable staying in that past place, it is actually up to you to close the door and move on to the new future in front of you.

Do you want to be stuck in the same-ol'-same-ol' phase of life? Or, do you want something completely different than what you had before?

I know you love those folks from your past. They are some of the best (or worst) friends you have ever had. But, just what part will they play in your future? **Will** they play a part in your future? It's just a thought.

It's up to you who you allow to travel with you on this new journey to the future. You see, not everyone can go with you where you are going. Not everyone *wants* to go with you!

When Apostle Paul said, "...*forgetting those things which are behind,*" he intimated that people and places were part of those things. There are some places you can't afford to revisit because the activities in those places could be detrimental to your forward movements. Although revisiting those places seems innocent on the surface, by digging deeper you will discover underlying activities, destruction waiting for you.

The destruction of your self-image, self-worth, hopes, dreams and desires awaits if you go back into what you have been released from. But, you have to *want* to be released from those places. Let me share a sad story with you.

This is a true but very, very sad story. Almost 20 years ago when our family resided in Kentucky, I served as pastor of a small congregation of born-again, Holy Ghost-filled believers. We were assigned to visit and minister in nursing homes, personal care facilities and Western State Mental Hospital. I met a young woman at Western State who really tugged at my heartstrings.

Her name doesn't matter (we'll call her Carrie); neither does her race. We ministered to every sex, race, color and creed in that facility.

Carrie* and I were around the same age with similar backgrounds; there the similarities ended. Carrie* had been in and out of mental institutions from the age of 12 or so. Yes; you read right – 12. She had been diagnosed with bi-polar disorder, schizophrenia, and other mental illnesses and instabilities from the age of 12.

When she and I met in our 30s, she was pretty much well-institutionalized; she was quite comfortable in Western State. As I ministered to this young woman, though, she began to change. The more we talked, the more her mannerisms and countenance changed; everything about her slowly changed.

Pretty soon, she began to voice her desire to leave Western State; she wanted a different life.

My congregation and I began to fast and pray for this young woman. I lay at the altar of Almighty God and made a covenant with Him; if He would release Carrie from Western State, I would give up caffeine.

Now, that may not seem like much to you. At the time, I was an avid black tea drinker. First thing in the morning and for most of the day, I drank tea. But, for Carrie to be released from the bondage of mental illness that had held her for so long, I was willing to give up drinking that black and orange pekoe tea.

I continued to visit Western State in anticipation of her release. Within two weeks, she was released! The state released her to a residential hotel near Western State Hospital. They needed to be able to keep track of her; she needed to be able to continue receiving state assistance until she regained her footing. We were ecstatic!

After her release, Carrie* called to ask if I could take her grocery shopping. When I went to the hotel to pick her up, she was a completely different person. Her mannerisms had changed. She actually smiled; and, it was genuine. She appeared to be happy for the first time since I had known her.

We went grocery shopping and had an awesome time! If you could have seen the look on Carrie's* face as she picked up each grocery item and placed it in her cart! I could tell that she was truly enjoying her freedom. And for about three weeks, she really did!

Unfortunately, she began to miss her friends at Western State. She longed for the atmosphere, the environment that had kept her hostage for so long. She missed the constancy of the nursing staff and the other patients (inmates) who had treated her so badly.

I couldn't understand it! You see, Carrie* called me periodically before her release and shared with me the patient abuse that went on in the hospital. At first, I thought she was delusional; surely a state-funded and run facility would not allow such blatant abuses to continually occur between the patients in their care! Unfortunately, I found that this was definitely the case.

My next door neighbor worked at Western State. He told me that Carrie* was telling the truth. He told me how the staff was powerless to stop the in-house abuses because their hands were shackled by the state! And she wanted to return?!?!

Carrie* wanted to go back to the people and place that would eventually destroy her. The end of her story, although she is still alive from the last I heard, is far sadder than the beginning.

Once she returned to Western State, she called to see if I would come and visit her. It broke my heart to tell her, *"No."*

You see, when the Lord released her from that particular season of her life, He also released me from having to visit Western State. Many of the patients my congregation and I had ministered to had been released from Western State and transferred to personal care facilities. Carrie* was the last.

The Lord had released Carrie* from Western State. He had prepared a new beginning for her; a new beginning which she threw back into His face. Although she plaintively pleaded with me, I could not go back to see her again at Western State Hospital.

You may wonder what happened with Carrie*. About seven or eight years ago, I contacted her Dad and Step-Mother. Their daughter not only reentered Western State Hospital, she was transferred to Central State Hospital in Louisville-Jefferson County, Kentucky. After killing a nurse, Carrie* was admitted to the criminally insane ward. Sadly, she will probably never be released from the mental institution.

Now, you may ask why Carrie* had such a hard time staying away from her P^3.A.S.T. Well, you need to understand just how comfortable your P^3.A.S.T. is.

In many cases, you have grown up with your P^3.A.S.T. During your formative years, all the habits you picked up, your quirks and idiosyncrasies developed in your P^3.A.S.T. The people, places and possibilities helped shape who you are up to a given point.

Once you became comfortable with the shape, it was hard for you to break out of that mold!

Your life is like a bowl of jello that has not yet congealed. As certain areas of your life harden or congeal, the only way anything new is introduced is if you push it into the gel. But, it does not really become a part of that gel as much as the gel surrounds and captures it.

As you go through the seasons of life, you gel into the purpose and destiny for your life. During the process, new things are introduced. Now, because many of these things are not part of your divine destiny or purpose, when they are introduced or pushed down into you, they became a part of you. However, they do not conform to the gelling action in your being.

At certain points in your life, you tend to come apart. In a sense, you are just like jello that has sat outside the refrigerator for too long and melts down. Although the components that caused you to congeal are still present, the conditions for your staying congealed have changed. You must get back to the place in which you can maintain your shape.

Now, how interesting is that? Carrie* had been given a chance to be molded into what God truly wanted her to be. He allowed her to be released from Western State so He could mold her into something completely different from the mold the world had poured her into. When released from Western State, she was placed in a situation around people in a place giving her greater possibilities than ever before.

But, she wanted to go back. When she went back, she fell apart and the un-congealing process took place in her life.

Have you revisited those people, places, possibilities and situations that should be terminated from your life? Have you found yourself stepping back in time instead of going forward into what your Creator has purposed for you?

If so, understand that you need to resist revisiting those people, places, possibilities and situations that should remain terminated because they will usually lead to your destruction.

In the last chapter, we created and worked with your **File Cabinet of Life ®**. Let's take this experience a step further.

Go back into your *File Cabinet* and pull out a particularly painful file from your youth. Let me give you an example from my life.

When I was four years old, I was in a pre-school/pre-kindergarten type situation in a private setting. The teacher was excellent! What I never told anyone was that her teen son molested me on a continuous basis at the time. This act scarred me for many years.

I went back to my *File Cabinet*, pulled up this file and walked with it. After completing a 360° turn, I decided that, although this is a reality, it is not my reality. I crumpled that reality and threw it into the **Round File of Life ®.** It will burn with today's refuse; I am finished with it!

OK. Are you ready? Do you have the file I asked for? In the spirit, hold that file up. Walk with it. See it and experience it for the last time. Walk your 360° turn.

As I write this, I want you to know that I am doing the same things I tell you to do. I have also had my youngest daughter do the same and she is excited by the results.

As you complete your circuit, crumple that file as small as you can and toss it into your **Round File**; it will be burned with the other refuse at the end of the day.

How do you feel? Do you feel the weight lifting? As I wrote this and completed the exercise myself, I attempted to go back to see if there was anything left of that episode in the corners of my mind. There wasn't! It's gone and I can move on past that!

So can you! You do not have to revisit that part of your P³.A.S.T. anymore. It's done! It's gone!

Move forward and clean out the rest of your **File Cabinet of Life ®!**

REMINDER:

D.S.ofL. Let Go of the Past Key #6

I have the power to change the outcomes in my life.

Your past does not have power over you. Your past is merely a moment in time through which you lived. Although it exists, it is only a vapor; vapors dissipate.

You have the power to change all outcomes in your life. Don't waste your time revisiting your past hoping that it will change itself. Change your view of past events; change the dynamic.

Change the outcomes of your life. Watch Almighty God do some of the most amazing things in and through your life; more than you ever imagined!

Chapter 13 – Press Toward The Mark

I invite you to consider the ironing process. When you are tasked with ironing an article of clothing like a shirt or a table cloth or a handkerchief, think about the process you have to go through.

<u>First</u>, you set up the ironing board. Now, I don't know about you, but I find ironing to be the most tedious of all tedious tasks I have ever had to accomplish. I learned to loathe ironing while serving in the Army. Have you ever had to starch a set of BDUs? ...Tedious to say the least. So, when I set up to iron, I make sure something good is on the TV or I put a movie in. Location; location; location!

<u>Secondly</u>, add cold water to the iron if you are going to use steam. When I was a child, we didn't have a steam iron. We had to sprinkle whatever we ironed to give it the same effect. We also used powdered starch mixed with water. We sprinkled handkerchiefs and shirts with this mixture.

So, now you turn on the iron so it can reach the proper temperature for optimal results.

Did I mention that back in the day we actually used a cast-iron iron that was heated on the wood stove? We never actually knew the temperature but were careful after much training from Mama to test the iron so we didn't scorch the fabric.

Lastly, if you haven't already done this, you gather the articles you will attack with the iron. You may set them in order from the most difficult to the easiest to press.

So, let's get started with what should be the least difficult, say, a handkerchief. I remember Mama ironing those square pieces of white cotton for Daddy. She starched every one of them and they came out crisp. Then, she folded each of them into 3"x3" squares for Daddy to carry in his pocket.

Now, the first thing you will notice as you begin the pressing process is the condition of the handkerchief as you place it on the ironing board: wrinkled, much wrinkled. As a matter of fact, you probably have to force it to lay as flat as possible as you prepare to put the iron to it.

But notice what happens as you begin to press it with that warm or hot iron. What happens to that wrinkled material? It begins to flatten out and becomes straight and crisp; just the way you want it.

Now, what is it that's wrinkled in your life? To be honest, as I look back over my past, I see nothing but wrinkles. Most of the wrinkles, I remember. I remember them as I went through each one; as I tried to make sense and press through each of them. I obviously did not understand the pressing process as I went through.

Throughout much of this book, we have focused on you forgetting those things which are behind, reaching toward those things in front of you, forgiving yourself and others you feel have wronged you. Now, we are going to press into your future as never before.

You need to understand that you must be as the iron for your journey ahead; it may be wrinkled. You must press forward and into your future so it will be sharp and crisp and have the appearance of what you desire it to be.

As the iron of your own life, of your own destiny, you have to heat up to the task ahead. Some of the tasks you face require a warm iron. There is not much resistance and the material of that situation takes to a moderately warm iron. You will also find in this situation that you don't need much starch and the pressing of this situation is almost effortless.

Not all that you face will be this easy. And that's a good thing! You need to exercise your pressing talents for those more pressing needs to come.

There are some tasks requiring a hotter iron. These situations are a bit more challenging, a bit more difficult to tame, if you will.

When I first entered the Army, we wore the OD Green fatigues. Those uniforms were very simple to press and really accepted the starch and a moderately hot iron. It didn't take long to press each suit and they always looked sharp with a pair of spit-shined boots.

When the Army introduced the Battle Dress Uniform (BDU), ironing became very, very tedious. You see, BDUs had pockets where there should not have been pockets, seams where they were the most annoying created in a really heavy, cotton material. It took almost twice as much time to iron a set of BDUs versus half the time for a set of fatigues.

The BDU was a totally different ironing animal. In life, you will find that you have fatigue situations and you have BDU situations. Now, BDUs always required steam and starch in order to give a razor-sharp appearance.

One thing I discovered about BDUs is that they act better when I returned them to the dryer for a bit before I ironed them; they were a bit more pliable.

Some of the situations you find yourself in will need to be put back in the Dryer of Life to knock out some of the wrinkles before you can move on with the pressing process.

But, *you* have to decide what process you will use. You have to decide how hot or warm you are going to be as you press forward to that destiny you know you were created for.

How do you feel today? The reason I ask is this: the way you press toward your mark of excellence today is determined by the inner dealings you may have with yourself at any given moment. Let me explain.

Say today one of your confidantes comes to you while you are working on a project. This person exuberantly, enthusiastically encourages you and helps you see your vision as not only viable but doable; not only doable but probable; not only probable but possible.

As this person bumps your faith in yourself and your vision up another notch, you get so excited that you start pressing through previous issues at a rate you never imagined! Not only do you press through your issues, you are ready to take on the seemingly insurmountable issues you had previously dealt with. You now have a new-found goal to do what needs to be done so you can get to where you need to get to!

You feel so good on the inside that you press toward the mark with a new measure of excellence. And people notice! Your business or work associates catch the fire and their vision for your life is caught and they run with it. You are running with your vision because you are pressing toward the mark for the high calling of excellence in your life.

On the other hand… we do have two, you know.

Say today one of your naysayers comes to speak with you about your vision. He or she tells you how much they wish well for you; but…

Your plan will never work…

Didn't you file bankruptcy several years ago? Isn't that still on your record?

What if you fail… again?

Just who do you think you are anyway? Many have tried this same thing but none have succeeded! Neither will you!

As this person continues to spiritually deflate you, your pressing strategy changes. You turn the heat down on the iron. You leave off the starch and steam because the wrinkles are going to be there anyway; right?

Your inner self no longer lines up with excellence. It is discouraged by all the negatives it has been told. And now, you run with what you have been told.

The Drill Sergeant of Life says: Get Over Yourself and Let Go Of the P³.A.S.T!

Release the naysayers and the Doomsday Speakers from your life! They don't mean well for you! If anything, they continually attempt to drag you back into the morass of mediocrity you were in before. Move forward whether they are with you or not!

MORE PROBING QUESTIONS

1.	Since beginning this process of letting go of the past, what past events, places or people have presented themselves that let you know you have to let them go?
2.	What are some of the past situations or circumstances now presenting themselves as wrinkles that you need to press out of your life?
3.	Are you warm or hot as you press these things out of your life?

Now, you may wonder what determines the temperature setting of your life as you press these things out?

As I told you, when I first became a soldier in 1977, the first uniform I wore was the OD Green fatigues. The process for ironing this uniform was pretty much straightforward. There were only a few creases that had to be ironed to give a sharp appearance. But, oh what an appearance!

As I also told you, though, BDUs were a totally different challenge. I had to use more starch and a higher temperature to achieve a similar result as with the fatigues.

Are you attempting to press out the wrinkles in the situations in your life with the same temperature you use for less difficult situations? The situations you previously had were easier than what you find yourself in now. You have to determine the fabric of your situation in order to know the amount of heat, steam, and starch needed to give it the sharp, crisp appearance you desire to have.

As you press toward the mark of your desired destination, these are some of the things you need to concentrate on. As you let go of the past, you also let go of the ways you previously dealt with your past.

Press on and knock out those wrinkles!

D.S.ofL. Let Go Of The Past Key #7

I press toward the mark of excellence with consistency and persistency.

Pressing toward the mark of excellence can only be accomplished by using various temperatures that are correct for the situation you are in. You will not use the same temperature with every situation you find yourself in.

As you press toward the mark of excellence, make sure you read the manufacturer's advice on the material you happen to be dealing with at the time. You may find that the fabric of the situation or circumstance can stand a hotter iron and more force than what you have been giving it.

Chapter 14 – Look at Jesus

This book is not about religion or your belief system. It is about faith. You see, you have to have faith in order to be able to let go of your past and move forward into your future. Jesus is the best example I know for moving from His past into His future.

To the people of His day, and even today, Jesus' life was questionable. Do you know that his lineage included a harlot, a liar and a... virgin?

I know; many folks have probably either said, *Whatever!* Or, *Yeah, right!!!* to Mary's claim of virginity prior to Jesus' birth. What would you have said if someone shared this story with you of a virgin birth? Would you be doubtful? ...Skeptical? Would you ridicule the bearer of the news? Would you believe any of it?

There are many skeptical people in the world. The closer Jesus came to the Cross of Calvary, His defining moment, He faced ridicule, hatred, anger and myriad betrayals and unbridled unbelief.

His earthly father (or, should I say stepfather?) was a carpenter. Surely the King of Kings would not be a simple carpenter for goodness sake! He was the eldest of several brothers and sisters who thought He was crazy for thinking that He was the Son of God. Yet...

Jesus turned water into wine. Now, think about this: no one really had a problem with Him turning the water into wine. I mean, we all want to have a good time; right? We all want to have a good time so it doesn't really matter who supplies the joy juice; right?

Although His mother Mary may have had doubts about His divinity up until this point, she always held in her heart the circumstances surrounding His conception. So you see, from before His birth, Jesus' past was wrought with persecution.

Upon His birth, King Herod plotted to kill all male Hebrew children two years of age and under. Herod had heard the rumors of the soon-coming king. He wanted to make sure that He did not get to take his place. But, Almighty God had a plan for Jesus, God-Incarnate.

So, His parents took Him to safety giving Him a chance in life; that did not stop the persecutors. That did not stop the unbelief. That did not stop a past fraught with questions that would follow Jesus for hundreds, thousands of years.

But, Jesus had to press forward in the face of persecution and mockery; He knew His purpose for coming to the earth. He knew the gifts and callings on His life. He knew what He would do before it was all said and done.

Now, I know you think that your life is nothing like Jesus' life. After all, He was God in the flesh on the earth according to the Holy Scriptures. He died for the sin of the world also according to the Holy Scriptures.

But, you have faced all kinds of persecution, ridicule, animosity, and hatred from various haters. But, you know you have a calling on your life. You know you have a mission to fulfill in this life. You have to forget... You have to forgive... You have to release all those who have been against you.

Sounds important, doesn't it? Almost sounds like something you really don't want to do, right? OK, then, let me rephrase: if you want to get over yourself and let go of the past, you need to forget... You need to forgive... You need to release all those who have been against you.

You need to look at the example of Jesus... Or, whomever you use as an example of letting go of the past. Gandhi... Mother Teresa... Churchill...

On the cross, Jesus prayed, *"Forgive them Father for they know not what they do!"*

Even on the cross, He forgave those who perpetrated a fraud against Him. He willingly looked past their faults and saw their need to be forgiven.

Do you have that same capacity? Can you look past your anger, hurt, and pain? Can you look at your haters with forgiveness in your heart, forgive and move on?

About 20 years ago, I had the opportunity to forgive all those who had done something to me at some point in my life. To be perfectly honest, I don't think I *wanted* to forgive them as much as I **needed** to forgive them.

The longer I held on to the hurt, anger, and pain in my heart, the more I allowed them to take control of my life. You see, it's all about control.

When others persecute you, no matter how brief the occurrence, if you allow those emotions to embrace you and you embrace them, those perpetrators control you. After all, when you are angry with someone and hold that person in your heart with anger, who are you really hurting?

Does it make sense for you to be the only one in pain because the other person has moved on in his or her life? Does it make sense for you to be sick over something that can easily be remedied?

You see, when Jesus asked the Father to forgive those who persecuted Him, it took all the pressure from Him, He was able to enter the Throne Room of Grace with no other thoughts than taking the sin of the world on His shoulders.

It makes no sense for you to bear the brunt of hurt feelings, anger and pain when all you need to do is forgive and move on.

I have an acquaintance who periodically suffers from hives. When she gets frustrated or upset by something someone else has said or done to her, she becomes ill and hives appear in various places on her body.

One day she called me about a situation she was dealing with. After hearing her story, I told her that maybe she was taking too much to heart and needed to let this garbage go.

"Why are you sick and the other person has moved on?" I asked.

She considered it for a moment and agreed with what I said. Why should she suffer when the other person was not even concerned? It was quite possible that the other person didn't even know the emotions my acquaintance was suffering through?

One of the major examples we can take from Jesus' lifetime on the earth is the ability to move forward in the face of opposition. Many times, He actively ministered to other people by healing their diseases and delivering them from various illnesses. Many people were so afraid of the gifts Jesus possessed they rejected Him and His gifts.

Instead of becoming angry with them and turning their rejection into anger, He simply walked away. That's all; He walked away from their rejection, the words of hatred, envy, jealousy, and animosity. He never said a word.

Even when He was betrayed, arrested, and beaten by the soldiers, He never uttered any words of anger or contempt to His persecutors.

How much strength does it take to be able to walk the path of forgiveness? How much energy will a person use when they are in the process of keeping their emotions from flaring when they have every right to be angry, upset, hurt, or...

Jesus is not the only Christian leader who has been persecuted; merely just the most prominent. He practiced what He preached. Consider Martin Luther King, Jr. and others who were martyred for their faith.

But, what if Jesus had really given thought to His persecutors in a negative way? What if, instead of praying, *"Forgive them Father,"* He prayed, *"Father, look at what they have done to Me!"*

In praying the way He prayed, Jesus was able to rid Himself of any hard feelings or vengeful thoughts in His heart and mind. He was able to go forth and save the world through His sacrifice.

Now, whatever you have been through, release it. Give it to the Father so you can move on and do what you have been called to do without regrets or remorse.

The next time you encounter those who persecute or ridicule you, take the high road of forgiveness. But, not only do you forgive, forget their transgression as much as possible so that it does not bog you down and cause you to be sick just from holding it in your heart.

Can you imagine how much better you will feel? Can you also imagine how much more effective you will be because you have learned the fine art of letting go of the past and grabbing hold of the future?

Let's face it; we are not equipped to continually carry the loads and burdens others so willingly place upon us. As a matter of fact, we have to consciously rid ourselves of those unwanted burdens so they don't drive us crazy.

And the only way to consciously rid ourselves of those unwanted burdens is to **Get Over Ourselves and Let Go of the P³.A.S.T.** If you will make an effort and go through each of the steps I have given you in this book, you will find that your productivity will increase and you will become more effective in everything you do. You will feel better about you and not need as much affirmation from others around you.

You will be able to define yourself and not have to wait for others to define you. You are an awesome individual! ***Get Over Yourself and Let Go Of The Past*** that continually attempts to hold you down!

REMINDER:

D.S.ofL. Let Go of the Past Key #7

I press toward the mark of excellence with consistency and persistency!

Is it easy to let go of the past and grab hold of your future? No! As a matter of fact, this will probably be the hardest thing you have ever done for yourself.

But, as you press toward the mark of excellence with consistency and persistency, you will find ways to make the road easier and the journey more conducive to your success.

Take the high road of forgiveness and let others see that you are striving for excellence and not mediocrity.

Chapter 15 – Have Faith in God! Have Faith in YOU!

You may wonder why I speak about Almighty God so much. You see, I don't know about Buddha, Krishna, or any other deities. I only know Jesus Christ and Him crucified. I know that I once was lost but now I'm found; I was blind but now I see.

You see, Almighty God was the Only One Who accepted me when everyone else rejected me. He is the Only One who loved me in spite of me when I was the most unlovable. He is the Only One Who has given me more chances than I deserve when others completely wrote me off. And He continually gives me chances; even when I mess up!

When I was at my lowest, God through Jesus Christ brought me higher than I have ever been before. Now, what you know, you know. But this is what I know. My good friend and mentor, Joe Sabah, advises *"Write and speak about what you know!"* Therefore, this is what I write and speak about.

And let me tell you about the low points! When I began the true journey of getting over myself, getting out of my own way so I could get what I wanted out of life, I was at a very decided low point. I was so sick of me, sick of my situation that I didn't know what to do.

It seemed as though my husband and I were constantly starting over. At the beginning of the 2000s, we filed for bankruptcy, lost our home to foreclosure and placed our two youngest children with family members so we could drive team for a trucking company. We had nothing but a will to survive. And, honestly, sometimes that is just not enough.

We both believed in God through Jesus Christ. We both prayed. It seemed as though nothing really worked the way we wanted it to. But, we were survivors. We plugged on and worked our tail ends off to provide for our family.

I went to Real Estate school, got my license; still nothing. The only money I made in Real Estate was from helping a fellow Realtor on a project and a referral commission when some friends moved to Arizona. I had other clients but nothing ever really came through.

In December 2008, we had to short-sell our home and move into our eldest daughter's basement. My husband continued to drive the truck and I continued to attempt to make money as a Realtor. Nothing. I turned in my Jeep Commander because I couldn't pay for it.

Then, in November 2009, the call came from my Dad; he needed me to come to NY to help him while he had a series of eye surgeries.

I was ready for a change anyway. I was discouraged, disheartened and tired. I couldn't make sense of anything. I had to find an answer but never expected the answer to come in the way it did.

As I prepared to go to New York to help Dad, I honestly thought I would only be there for three maybe six months. I never imagined being away from my husband, children and home for over a year!

The day my oldest daughter and I got on the plane, everything changed. My daughter traveled with me because she wanted to check on her granddad for herself. Settling on the plane, she asked a question that I immediately knew meant something else was happening besides what I was initially travelling for.

*"Mom, you **do** know Grandma's cancer came back, right?"*

All I could do was look at my daughter; I did not know that my biological mother's cancer had returned. At this point, all bets were off; **God had set me up!** There was much more going on than I had ever expected.

Once we arrived in NY, nothing went as I had planned; but, everything went according to God's plan for me.

My mother began her last season on the earth. She began frequent visits back and forth to the hospital around December 15 or so. As for my Dad's surgery, wires were crossed and the first of two surgeries was scheduled around January 28. The second surgery was a month later; so much for me only being there for three months, six for that matter.

But I made the best of a not-necessarily-good, not-necessarily-bad situation. On my 51st birthday, I went to 42nd street to see a movie. I think it was a movie with Denzel Washington. I spent several hours roaming the streets of Manhattan by myself; something I had never done before. I learned to travel on the subway without getting lost.

When Mom went into the hospital for what would be the last time, I was able to leave my Dad's apartment at 7am, get to the hospital by 8:30 am or so and stay until one of my siblings came in the evening and I could go home until the next day.

Now, understand; I didn't do this to get anyone's attention. I didn't do what I did, as some supposed, to curry any special favor from my biological mother whom I barely knew. I did it because I filled a need. I also did it so I could get to know this woman who had given birth to me.

During a period of a little over a year, I had to learn to trust my Creator, Father God, the God of Abraham, Isaac and Jacob, Jehovah God. I was thousands of miles away from home, forced to live in a place in which I really wasn't wanted (a long story) taking care of someone I barely knew.

I had no job, very little income, and was practically in a foreign land amid foreigners (New Yorkers are very foreign to me and I love them all!)

During my time in New York, I also came to know not only my biological mother as she went through the final throes of cancer, but, also my siblings with whom I did not grow up. I was able to be there for and with her when she breathed her final breath.

I had to trust God that He would use me to minister to my family; both sides. On my Dad's side, I was able to connect with family members I had grown up with but lost contact. On my Mom's side, I was able to connect with and learn more about my four brothers and two sisters that I had not grown up with. I was able to minister to them as the Lord saw fit.

I had to trust God that He knew what He was doing in my life; I sure didn't!

I had to trust God that He was working out all things in my life for His glory and for my good. I couldn't see what He saw in my situation. I definitely could not see the big picture: I just had to trust Him.

I had to trust and have faith in Him as never before as I stayed in New York away from my beloved husband and children. I had to keep encouraged because, to be honest, my situation was very discouraging.

And it was not easy! There were countless days in which I cried and prayed to be released from my exile. But the Lord was determined to walk this thing out in me.

Many of you are probably confused by my experience in this season of my life. Many of you probably think it wrong that a wife and mother be pulled away from husband and children to go on such a journey. But, you need to understand the Lord; you must understand my relationship with Him.

I prayed and cried. I fasted, prayed and cried. I wrote journal page after journal page as God downloaded into my Spirit. I listened to His voice inside my heart. I read His loving words. I ingested and digested everything He said to me. I received the many revelations He opened to me. I traveled the road He laid out before me.

I embarked on this *God-journey* to find the *'Beatrice'* He had created me to be.

He showed me how to let go of my past and grab hold of my future. He would not let me go!

There were times I stayed in my bedroom at my Dad's apartment for days on end not worrying about going out or seeing any other faces.

I prayed; oh, how I prayed as God revealed more and more to me!

I listened to His voice. I came to know His voice as one of the sheep that remains close to the shepherd. I heard Him; He heard me. We communed as never before!

As I came to trust Him completely, He taught me to trust... myself. He taught me to have faith in the gifts He had placed within me. He taught me to flow in those gifts.

Oh, what an incredible journey this has been! I no longer look at my past with fear and trepidation. Because of the faith I have in Almighty God, I now have faith in the gifts He has bestowed upon me. I have faith in the fact that I can do what He has called me to do. I have faith in Him because of His faithfulness!

Have I told you that God is FAITHFUL!!! Oh, yes He is!!! You see, He faithfully restores each and every one of us to Himself on a daily basis. He renews His compassions for us and extends them to us on a daily basis. He is faithful when we are faithless!

As I said before, this book is not about religion. It is about letting go of your past so you can grab hold of the future that God has in store for you.

So, have faith in God. Have faith in yourself. Let go of your past, the P³.A.S.T. that hinders you from the awesome future in front of you.

You can do it! You gots what it takes! Gets What you Wants!

I have faith in you! More importantly, God has faith in you!

The Drill Sergeant

D.S.ofL. Let Go of the Past Key Recap

1. I'm not perfect but I'm willing.

2. My future apprehends and challenges me! I apprehend and challenge my future!

3. I don't have it yet; but I'm getting it.

4. This one thing I do: I choose TODAY to let go of the past.

5, I am not my past. Therefore, I forget those things behind me and move forward in my destiny and purpose.

6. I have the power to change the outcomes in my life.
7. I press toward the mark of excellence with consistency and persistency.

APPENDIX A

FIND MY PURPOSE QUESTIONNAIRE

CHILDHOOD

1.	What was your favorite thing to do as a child? Why?
2.	What was the main activity your parent(s) had to tell you to stop doing to go to bed most/every night(s)?

3. What role-playing games did you enjoy as a child? I.e., teaching your pets, singing with a comb-microphone, styling your doll's hair, etc.

4. What book characters do you remember and identify with most from childhood? Why?

5. What did you want to be when you grew up? Why?

MIDDLE/JUNIOR/HIGH SCHOOL

1.	In which subject(s) did you excel? Why?
2.	What type people were you drawn to and were drawn to you? Why?

3. In which sports or other extracurricular activities did you participate? Why?

4.	Which sports or extracurricular activities gave you the greatest pleasure? Why?
5.	Who was your favorite role-model in High School? Why?

6. From career search evaluations you participated in, what was your most likely career following High School and College?

7. What was your first job in high school? What did you

	like about it?
8.	What were your plans after high school? College? Military? Job Corp?

COLLEGE/MILITARY

1.	If you attended college, what was the burning desire that sent you there? Why?
2.	What was your major or minor? Why?

3. Was this your choice or the choice of your parents, guardian, or mentor? Why?

4.	What did you do with that major or minor? Why?
5.	Are you currently working in the field of your studies? Are you enjoying yourself? Why? Why not?

6. If you opted for the military, what was your specialty?

7. Are you currently working in your specialty or field of study? Why? Why not?

8. Do you enjoy what you are doing? Why? Why not?

PRESENT DAY

1.	Do you feel that your life is over and it is too late to change the dynamics? Why?
2.	What is your current occupation? Do you **honestly** enjoy yourself?

3.	What is the burning desire for your life right now? Why?

4.	What do you love doing that causes you to lose track of time? Why?
5.	What gift or talent do most people come to you for and compliment you on?

6.	What do you think about doing most? Why?
7.	Would you do this for free?

8.	How much time, effort, money are you willing to spend on fulfilling your purpose?

9.	How important is it to you to fulfill your purpose in life?
10.	Are you ready to change the dynamic in your life? Why? Why Not?

11.	What do you see for your life right now?
12.	After you **Get Over Yourself,** where do you see yourself within the next year? Three years? Five Years?

BONUS QUESTION

If you knew this was your last day of life, what would be the first thing you would do? (Quit your job, go on vacation, etc.)

APPENDIX B

File Cabinet of Life ®

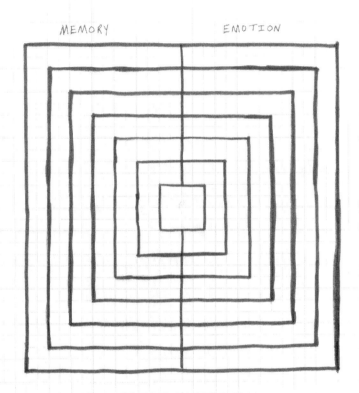

THE FILE CABINET OF LIFE

MEMORY EMOTION

Copyright (c) 2012 BEATRICE BRUNO, THE DRILL Sergeant of LiR

ABOUT THE AUTHOR

Beatrice Bruno is a 15-year Active Duty Army Veteran but always and forever a Drill Sergeant! Having served in various assignments in the Army, Beatrice admits that "*being a Drill Sergeant was the most rewarding two years of my life!*"

A Born-again Christian and ordained Gospel Minister, Beatrice has mentored and counseled people in all stages of life. Serving in ministry for over 20 years, Beatrice has found that people from all walks of life have the same need: to get over self and let go of the past!

Working from both sides of the spectrum, Drill Sergeant and Minister, Beatrice has developed a simple, no-nonsense solution for letting go of the past and grabbing hole of the future and moving forward into the future for which you have been created.

Journey with the Drill Sergeant of Life as she emerges from exile into her purpose in assisting you to **Get Over Yourself and Let Go of the Past!**

If your group would like to purchase this book in bulk, please contact us at www.TheGetOverItGal.com.

If you would like to engage *The Drill Sergeant of Life* to speak at your conference or event, please contact her at 720-212-9780 or Beatrice@TheGetOverItGal.com.

CHECK YOUR LEADING BOOKSTORE OR ORDER HERE

YES, I want _____ copies of *How To Get Over Yourself and Let Go of the P.A.S.T.!* at $20.00 each, plus $4 shipping per book (Colorado residents please add $1.75 sales tax per book.) Canadian orders must be accompanied by a postal money order in U.S. funds. Allow 15 days for delivery.

My check or money order for $_____ is enclosed. Please charge my Visa _____, MasterCard _____, Discover _____ or American Express _____.

Name _____

Organization _____

Address _____

City/State/Zip _____

Phone _____ Email _____

Card # _____ Exp. Date _____

Signature _____   _____

Please make check payable and return to:

The Drill Sergeant of Life

PO Box 350253

Westminster, CO 80035

21497868R00102

Made in the USA
Charleston, SC
19 August 2013